Proverbs
A Book of Wisdom
for Boys

Proverbs 1-11
A Devotional for
Pre-Teen Boys

Paul Sutliff

Michael Williams

ISBN: 9781672418041

For the boys in Hope Christian Fellowship! Press on to become the young men of God that you are called to be.

With love,

Your Teachers

ABOUT THE AUTHORS

 **Paul Sutliff** – Paul is a father of three grown children now in their 20s. He works as a Special Education Teacher and a writer. Paul came to know the Lord as his savior, when he was 16. Paul credits a lot of his own wisdom in this world to his father, who taught him things like, "You are responsible for what you know." Paul loves worship and teaching young adults about Apologetics.

 **Michael Williams** – Michael says he was a rebellious teen. He wanted to run in the streets like his older brothers. His mother wanted to keep him safe at home. Michael experimented with drugs and became addicted not long after. Michael found Jesus and entered a drug rehab program. There he met Pastor Robert Frazer and his wife Juanita. They adopted Robert not legally but with their love. Pastor Frazer passed on his love of music to Michael who now plays bass on the worship team and sings an occasional solo with the choir.

INTRODUCTION

King Solomon, the wisest king on the earth once was inspired by God to write down the wise and smart things he wished his kids to know. Well, at least he wanted his sons to know. Because, when you're the wisest guy on the planet, not everyone gets it. They only know you are the man with the answers. Wouldn't you like to be the guy people come to with questions expecting you to know the answer?

This little book of 31 chapters was written by a wise king, the wisest king so you, a boy, wouldn't grow up foolish. One of things the king is always talking about in this book is what fools do. Well of course, we don't want to be fools, do we? He tells us what good men or wise men do. Pretty simple, foolish = Bad. Wise = good.

Ready for the adventure? HERE WE GO!

DAY 1
PROVERBS 1:1-6

1 The proverbs of Solomon son of David, king of Israel:

2 for gaining wisdom and instruction; for understanding words of insight;

3 For receiving instruction in prudent behavior, doing what is right and just and fair;

4 for giving prudence to those who are simple, knowledge and discretion to the young--

5 let the wise listen and add to their learning, and let the discerning get guidance—

6 for understanding proverbs and parables, the sayings and riddles of the wise.

As I wrote this for you, I stopped and thought about the word "prudence." How do I explain this to the boys? So, I looked it up not once but twice. Then I started to chuckle. Why? Because King Solomon had a way with words that makes older men laugh. He wrote this for boys in many ways. He wrote it for boys before they became older like me.

So, "for giving prudence" means what? Prudence means "common sense." There are some people born without it. King Solomon calls them the simple. As you get older you are going to find that funny. What is "common sense?" Common sense is that voice within you that says immediately, "I SHOULD DO THIS!" or, "I better not, Mom will be mad if I do this." It's the voice that just knows. A lot of times it's just that easy. The voice inside just knows. Admit it, most of you know what I am talking about. If you don't have that voice---well, then you are the simple King

Solomon is talking about. But he didn't forget about you. Because he is trying to give you "common sense" by writing this book. Pretty cool!

"Discretion" is a word that describes knowing how to behave. Some things you have to learn by doing the wrong thing and then be corrected. Or, as I say to boys, sometimes you have to do the stupid thing to learn the wise thing, the better thing. Discretion is when you have achieved it and gone beyond the stupid thing. This wise guy, this wise King, wants you to know things without having to do learn from doing the stupid things. WAY COOL!

What do you have to do? Verse five and six tell you. Listen and learn. Sounds simple. Sounds easy. Wait is that all, really? YES!

Dear Jesus!

Thank you for having King Solomon write a book to share his wisdom. I so often do the stupid things I shouldn't, maybe this will help me do better. Help me to listen and learn so I may become wiser. So, I may be an example. Better yet, so I may become the bait that leads my friends and others to know who you are!

Thank you, Jesus for loving me.

Amen

DAY 2
PROVERBS 1: 7-9

7 The fear of the LORD [is] the beginning of knowledge: [but] fools despise wisdom and instruction.

8 My son, hear the instruction of thy father, and forsake not the law of thy mother:

9 For they [shall be] an ornament of grace unto thy head, and chains about thy neck.

When I think of fear, I think of things I am scared of like heights. When I was about your age the lights once went out. I still remember a toy I loved that I had on a shelf and when the lights went out became a scary thing to me. It would put shivers up my spine and cause me to fear getting out of bed.

Do you think that is what King Solomon meant by "fear of the Lord?"

Sometimes fear has to do with respect. You may not think about it, but you do fear making your mother or father disappointed. I still remember the pain in my father's face when he found out I signed his name on a practice slip that said I practiced my instrument 30 minutes a day when I hadn't.

Your mother and father want to give you every bit of wisdom that will make you better than they are today. They will say no to you about many things. "No you can't do that." "No you can't play with him." "No you can't go there." But then they say yes, a lot too. These are actual nuggets of wisdom you will store away and someday use.

Now each of you has a respect of God. HE is BIG! HE loves more than we do. HE loves us more than we can understand especially after we do the stupid things we do. So, we best try not to disappoint Him. Think about that as a golden nugget, that a secret stash of gold grows from.

That gold is the beginning of your knowledge, the beginning of your wisdom, the beginning of truly knowing who you are in the world.

Sounds like a whopper of a start. If it's hard to imagine not knowing who God is. You owe your mom and dad a hug for giving that gift to you!

That means you are listening to them. You don't dislike these little nuggets of wisdom they give to you. Oh, I know there are times you want to close your ears, you want to shut the door and stomp out the world. I did that! Your Mother and Father did it too!

Ornaments are the jewelry you see people wear. Think about that. That means by simply doing what your mother and father ask, you are making jewelry. Sounds silly somewhat right?

I found a story that makes me think of this in an old textbook from the 1860s.

There were three boys who never seemed to listen to their parents. Their moms and dads had told them the calm peaceful river out back was a VERY DANGEROUS RIVER. But the boys had swam in it almost since they could walk. They had fished and had run through the water's edge. They had splashed and played in the river every day since they could remember. To them it was a paradise. So, they built a raft to see their paradise.

After they finished building the raft all three boys jumped on. The river wasn't so wide they couldn't swim across. It was a very s-l-o-w river. So, they just knew it would be safe. Their parents had to be wrong, it couldn't be dangerous!

As they went out of sight of their homes, a man yelled, "Come ashore DANGER AHEAD!"

They laughed and laughed, what could he know.

The man got on his horse, the river then pulled a bit harder. It was like being on a carnival ride not too fast, they could see the bottom. They were watching the fish swim by. Paradise the boys told each other.

The man on his horse raced a little ahead, and he yelled louder, "COME ASHORE! DANGER AHEAD!"

The boys laughed and laughed. Who was this fool to tell them their paradise was dangerous?

He acted frantic, waving his arms and pointing ahead.

Suddenly the river turned. The slow, merry pace changed from the fun ride to a racing downhill sprint! Rocks jutted out of the water and at odd places the raft kept smashing into them. The boys were scared!

Will you make jewelry with listening to the wisdom of your parents, or will you be like the three boys above? That is a choice for you to make every day.

Dear Jesus,

Be the beginning of my knowledge. Start me on the right track. I may be foolish. I may often be wrong. Help me to listen to my Mom. Help me to listen to my Dad. Help me to remember I need their wisdom. And God, I ask you make my parents super smart so I can learn great things from them!

Thank you, Lord! In Jesus Name, Amen

DAY 3
PROVERBS 1: 10-19

10 My son, if sinful men entice you, do not give in to them.

11 If they say, "Come along with us; let's lie in wait for innocent blood, let's ambush some harmless soul;

12 let's swallow them alive, like the grave, and whole, like those who go down to the pit;

13 we will get all sorts of valuable things and fill our houses with plunder;

14 cast lots with us; we will all share the loot"--

15 my son, do not go along with them, do not set foot on their paths;

16 for their feet rush into evil, they are swift to shed blood.

17 How useless to spread a net where every bird can see it!

18 These men lie in wait for their own blood; they ambush only themselves!

19 Such are the paths of all who go after ill-gotten gain; it takes away the life of those who get it.

Some words in the book of proverbs are not used much today, like the word "entice." Try using the word "tempt" instead.

"My son, if sinful men tempt you, do not give in to them."

These 9 verses either have you saying, "NO WAY! That is not me!" or, they have you thinking things like "How bad can a robbers life be?"

Bullies like a crowd. They like followers. "Come along with us..." Only today they say things like, "You can hang with us. We will make you safe. We won't let anyone hurt you." Doesn't sound like a bully? You're right!

But you probably have an idea of who I am talking about. The guys who hang outside just a little later than your mom and dad want you outside. The guys who brag about the things they did during the weekend and as you listen, you think, "My mom or dad would kill me if I did that."

So here they are asking YOU to join them....

They do not start out saying "hang with us, we are going to rob the old man down the street. It will be cool. Join us and you will get your cut." No, they talk about how cool they are and how great it would be for you to hang out with them.

Once there was a boy named Chan, who did give in and go hang with the gang. It was cool. They treated him to little things, like sodas, candy, and more. Things mom and dad would say costs too much, or that wasn't good for him to have too much of. He felt special! COOL! He became part of their gang! Now it was his gang too!

As he hung with them, they would ask him to do little things like go grab a soda in the store without paying for it. Or, "Grab me a King-sized Snickers Bar." It seemed scary the first time. He was lucky though. He didn't get caught. But the third time he did. His mom and dad were embarrassed. They had to go to the police station to get their son who had disobeyed them and broken the law. He stayed home and listened to them for a while. But he kept thinking about the fun he had hanging out with the gang.

Chan was back hanging with them soon. He came in when they were talking about jumping the fat, old, blind man down the street. He was supposed to have money, because he was always nicely dressed. He had too much money for his own good. He should give it to them. It was all talk …

Then, Chan found himself walking down the street with the guys. The old, blind man came around the corner. The gang grabbed him and dragged him to a place they couldn't be seen.

The poor man quickly offered his wallet. It had $40 in it. "Where is the rest of it?" The blind man said he didn't know what they were talking about. They began to punch and beat him demanding more. The old man cried, begging God for help. A siren sounded and the gang split. They ran in all different directions.

The sad thing about this story is it happened to one of my teachers when I was in college. He was older, blind, and yes, fat. He had a smile and love of God that made people happy to know him. I was not his student, but I ran into him every day. He always had some wisdom to share with me.

I still remember the days I visited him in the hospital. The first day I did not even recognize him. My whole being crying inside because I could not grasp the amount of pain he was in and still this man praised God. The boys who hurt him thought they could never be prosecuted. He could not identify them because he was blind. I heard they caught the boys later.

This story did not talk about blood being spilt. It didn't end with someone dying. But there are many that do.

Are you going to be the one who makes choices to seek wisdom and listens to mom and dad, or are you going to be the one listening to those who tempt you with what you know is wrong now?

Dear God,

Help me to make the right choices. I know I often choose to do the stupid things … things my parents are not proud of.

Please God, guide my feet. Lead me to make good choices, wise choices. So, I may be the bait that leads other to know you!

In your name, Amen.

DAY 4
PROVERBS 1:20-21 (NIV)

20 Out in the open wisdom calls aloud, she raises her voice in the public square;

21 on top of the wall she cries out, at the city gate she makes her speech

---

Proverbs was originally written in Hebrew. Sometimes when words get translated, they do not communicate all of what was intended by the author. It's accurate, but it's just missing something. In this case, the Hebrew word for wisdom actually refers to "wisdoms," "ways of human understandings." Humans – people, understand things like the stars, the ocean, the mountains, jungles, deserts, even some of outer space.

Think of this passage meaning GOD, calls to us through the wisdom of men. He announces Himself, not in secret, but in nature. In some sense the more you learn, the more you learn of God.

God calls not just to you and me, but to everyone! Think of this. God in His greatness does not want to leave one behind, so he announces Himself to everyone. He does not grab a megaphone and say, "HERE I AM," or "YES STUPID! I AM REAL." He gives us the chance to see HIM on our own. He lets this become personal for each and every one.

Think of this passage as you are looking into the night sky. Watching the stars -- no distraction, no sounds of cars or people passing by just beauty of the night sky. As you think about what you are seeing you think of how big the sky is and how much BIGGER God must be!

Then there are marvels in science. In a leaf, there are little machines that change sunlight into food. There are actual fountains under the sea! So many marvels! So many ways to see and hear God yelling to us "SEE ME! I AM HERE!"

But as time goes on you will meet people who play tricks on themselves insisting God is not real, and nothing is bigger than nature. I laugh when I hear this thinking of how small their idea of god is. Well, if that is their idea of god, they haven't met the GOD we serve. HE IS HUGE!

Dear God,

Please help me to see you announcing who you are today. I know you're a big God. Let me see how you announce who you are today.

Help me to be a good learner so I can gain understanding of this world and see you more. It's kind of cool, thinking of all the ways you tell people who you are. Jesus help me to see this.

Lord, also make me brave enough to share, when I do see you in what I learn.

Thank you, God for being sooo BIG!

In your name, Amen.

DAY 5
PROVERBS 1:22-33

22 "How long will you who are simple love your simple ways? How long will mockers delight in mockery and fools hate knowledge?

23 Repent at my rebuke! Then I will pour out my thoughts to you, I will make known to you my teachings.

24 But since you refuse to listen when I call and no one pays attention when I stretch out my hand,

25 since you disregard all my advice and do not accept my rebuke,

26 I in turn will laugh when disaster strikes you; I will mock when calamity overtakes you --

27 when calamity overtakes you like a storm, when disaster sweeps over you like a whirlwind, when distress and trouble overwhelm you.

28 "Then they will call to me, but I will not answer; they will look for me but will not find me,

29 since they hated knowledge and did not choose to fear the LORD.

30 Since they would not accept my advice and spurned my rebuke,

31 they will eat the fruit of their ways and be filled with the fruit of their schemes.

32 For the waywardness of the simple will kill them, and the complacency of fools will destroy them;

33 but whoever listens to me will live in safety and be at ease, without fear of harm."

When I think of this passage I am reminded of a classroom where the teacher tries to teach but the boys refuse to listen. They talk across the classroom. They talk of things no boy should talk of in public. They insult the teacher and laugh at him. The teacher tries and tries, not giving up. Doing everything to try to get through to the boys. The teacher even calls the boys' parents daily, but nothing changes. This goes on every day. It becomes tiring and the teacher begins to try less and less to get through to them. They never listen, and they have a wild time. But every day the teacher gives the lesson regardless if the boys will listen or not.

Then a test is given. All of the boys fail and blame the teacher for not teaching. Their parents call and blame the teacher. But the teacher reminds the parents and boys that there were daily calls home. There were many attempts to get the boys to listen. The cycle of refusing to learn and refusing to accept responsibility continued the entire year.

The boys only saw what they were doing as fun. They were not able to see the damage they were doing to themselves. The refusal to take part in learning made these boys a whole year behind their classmates in other classes.

Is this type of boy, the one who stands up for Jesus? NO! As boys, standing up for Jesus often means standing out. People see us for what we do and do not do. We should not be rude to our elders. We should be examples of how to respect those over us. We should be the good ones to our teachers, the ones who listen and give their best. The ones who study for tests. Why? Because we need to attain wisdom, knowledge and understanding. That is what God wishes for us!

Dear God,

I know I am often foolish. Please keep me from choosing to do the wrong things. Please keep me from choosing not to listen to my Mom and Dad or teachers.

Jesus, I need to do what is right. Help me to stand up for you by doing what is right. If I stand out, let it be You that is seen. Not me.

In Jesus Name, Amen.

DAY 6
PROVERBS 2:1-10 NIV

1 My son, if you accept my words and store up my commands within you,

2 turning your ear to wisdom and applying your heart to understanding—

3 indeed, if you call out for insight and cry aloud for understanding,

4 and if you look for it as for silver and search for it as for hidden treasure,

5 then you will understand the fear of the LORD and find the knowledge of God.

6 For the LORD gives wisdom; from his mouth come knowledge and understanding.

7 He holds success in store for the upright, he is a shield to those whose walk is blameless,

8 for he guards the course of the just and protects the way of his faithful ones.

9 Then you will understand what is right and just and fair--every good path.

10 For wisdom will enter your heart, and knowledge will be pleasant to your soul.

      The loving God we seek cares so much for you, that while you are trying to grow in His wisdom, HE protects you. How? Well the best way to explain this is that our God does impossible things. This is a poem I found in an old textbook. The rabbi is a seeker of wisdom. He reads God's Word every night to learn more about God and what he can and should do better. Pious means faithful.

The Four Misfortunes

By John G. Saxe

A Pious Rabbi, forced by heathen hate,
　　To quit the boundaries of his native land,
Wandered abroad submissive to his fate,
　　Through pathless woods and wastes of burning sand.

A patient ass, to bear him in his flight,
　　A dog, to guard him from the robber's stealth,
A lamp, by which to read the law at night, --
　　Was all the pilgrim's store of worldly wealth.

At set of sun he reached a little town,
　　And asked for shelter and a crumb of food;
But every face replied him with a frown,
　　And so he sought his lodging in the wood.

"'Tis very hard," the weary traveler said,
　　"And most inhospitable, I protest,
To send me fasting to this forest bed;
　　But God is good and means it for the best!"

He lit his lamp to read the sacred law,
　　Before he spread his mantle for the night;
But the wind rising with a sudden flaw,
　　He read no more,--the gush put out the light.

"'Tis strange," he said, "'tis very strange indeed,
　　That ere I lay me down to take my rest,
A chapter of the law I may not read,--
　　But God is good and all is for the best!

With these consoling words the rabbi tries

To sleep, --his head reposing on a log,--
But, ere he fairly shut his drowsy eyes,
    A wolf came up and killed his faithful dog.

"What new calamity is this?" he cried;
    "My honest dog – a friend who stood the test
When others failed – lies murdered at my side!
    Well, --God is good and means it for the best."
Scarce had the Rabbi spoken, when alas! –
    As if, at once, to crown his wretched his lot,
A hungry lion pounced upon the ass,
    And killed the faithful donkey on the spot.

"Alas!—alas!" the weeping Rabbi said,
    "Misfortune haunts me like a hateful guest;
My dog is gone, and now my ass is dead, --
    Well, God is good and all is for the best!"

At dawn of day, imploring heavenly grace,
    Once more he sought the town, but all in vain;
A band of robbers had despoiled the place,
    And all the churlish citizens were slain.

"Now God be praised!" the grateful Rabbi cried,
    "If I had tarried in this town to rest,
I too, with these poor villagers had died, --
    Sure, God is good and all is for the best!"

"Had not the saucy wind blown out my lamp,
    By which I read the sacred law I have read,
The light had shown the robbers to my camp,
    And here the villains would have left me dead.

"Had not my faithful animals been slain,

Their noise, no doubt, had drawn the robbers near,
And so their master, it is very plain,
Instead of them, had fallen murdered here.

"Full well I see that this has happened so
To put my faith and patience to the test;
Thanks to His name! For now I surely know
That God is good, and all is for the best!"

Dear God,
Help me to seek your wisdom. Help me to see how you protect
me. Give me the strength and ability to stand for you in all I do.

In Jesus name, Amen.

DAY 7
PROVERBS 2:11-14

11 Discretion will protect you, and understanding will guard you.

12 Wisdom will save you from the ways of wicked men, from men whose words are perverse,

13 who have left the straight paths to walk in dark ways,

14 who delight in doing wrong and rejoice in the perverseness of evil.

Discretion has two meanings. 1. To avoid behaving or speaking in such a way that would make people upset. 2. The freedom to choose what should be done in a certain situation.

Both of these meanings rely on your wisdom to make good choices.

But a Christian's wisdom starts with the fear of the Lord. It is different. We often see things slightly differently. Sometimes discretion means doing the right thing "just because."

Have you ever watched two people arguing. You listen to both sides, then all of a sudden one of them says something that makes you understand all of what is happening. When you get older "understanding" means you see through a situation. Somehow, just somehow, your experiences allow you to know exactly what is happening and how to deal with it.

I tend to get a smile on my face when I have an "understanding" moment. Why? Because something that could be confusing to others, I get! To be honest, at those times, I almost feel like dancing and singing "I know what is happening and what to do."

King Solomon and the Bees

By John Godfrey Saxe

When Solomon was reigning in his glory,
    Unto his throne the Queen of Sheba came,
(So in the Talmud you may read the story.)
    Drawn by the magic of the monarch's[1] fame,
To see the splendor of his court, and bring
Some fitting tribute[2] to the mighty king.

Nor this alone: much had her highness heard
    What flowers of learning graced the royal speech:
What gems of wisdom dropped with every word;
    What wholesome lessons he was wont to teach

---

[1] Def. king
[2] Def. gift

In pleasing proverbs; and she wished, in soothe,
To know if Rumor spoke the simple truth.

And straight she held before the monarch's view,
     In either hand, a radiant wreath of flowers;
The one, bedecked with every charming hue[3],
     Was newly culled[4] Nature's choicest bowers[5];
The other, no less fair in every part,
Was the rare product of divine Art[6].

"Which is true, and which is false?" she said.
     Great Solomon was silent. All amazed,
Each wondering courtier[7] shook his puzzled head,
     While at the garlands long the monarch gazed,
As one who sees a miracle, and fain,
For every rapture[8], ne'er would speak again.

"Which is true?" once more the woman asked,
Pleased at the fond amazement of the king;
"So wise a head should not be hardly taxed,
     Most learned liege[9], with a trivial thing."
But still the sage was silent,--it was plain
A deepening doubt perplexed the royal brain.

While thus he pondered, presently he sees
     Hard by the casement,--so the story goes,--
A little band of busy, bustling bees,

---

[3] Def. color
[4] Def. cut
[5] Def. climbing plant like ivy with flowers
[6] Def. man made
[7] Def. person who works in the King's court
[8] Def. Great joy
[9] Def. royal one over you

Hunting for honey in a withered rose.
The monarch smiled, and raised his royal head:
"Open the window!"—that was all he said.

The window opened at the king's command,
    Within the room the eager insects flew,
And sought the flower's in Sheba's dexter[10] hand!
    And so the king and all the courtiers knew
That wreath was Nature's; and the baffled queen
Returned to tell the wonders she had seen.

My story teaches (every tale should bare
    A fitting moral) that the wise may find
In trifles light as atoms in the air
    Some useful lesson to enrich the mind,
Some truth designed to profit or to please,--
As Israel's king learned wisdom from the bees!

Dear God,
I know you are not finished with me yet. Please work on me. Teach me wisdom, teach me knowledge, and help me to gain understanding. So, one day I may shine for you. By simply sharing the wisdom I have gained. You are truly a loving God!

In Jesus Name, Amen.

DAY 8
PROVERBS 2:12-22 NIV

12 Wisdom will save you from the ways of wicked men, from men whose words are perverse,

---

[10] Def. the right side

13 who have left the straight paths to walk in dark ways,

14 who delight in doing wrong and rejoice in the perverseness of evil,

15 whose paths are crooked and who are devious in their ways.

16 Wisdom will save you also from the adulterous woman, from the wayward woman with her seductive words,

17 who has left the partner of her youth and ignored the covenant she made before God.

18 Surely her house leads down to death and her paths to the spirits of the dead.

19 None who go to her return or attain the paths of life.

20 Thus you will walk in the ways of the good and keep to the paths of the righteous.

21 For the upright will live in the land, and the blameless will remain in it;

22 but the wicked will be cut off from the land, and the unfaithful will be torn from it.

God is willing to save you from men and women who will lead you astray and into a life of sin. There are some out there who rejoice in living a sinful life. They think doing sinful things is OK because it makes them feel good. You need to know that some people get physically ill from being sinful. They carry such sickness on them and have no issues with having you join them in their sickness, even if they know it will cause you to die.

This is another reason it is important to listen to your parents as you get older and start to date. Moms and Dads see things and know things because they have experienced life more than you. Better God has given you to them as a gift, so he often gives parents something special, called intuition [in-2-ition] that makes them pleased or concerned with who you are friends with.

Think of the last two verses. "The upright will live in the land, and the blameless will remain in it; but the wicked will be cut off from the land, and the faithful will be torn from it."

To do as God asks of you, to seek wisdom and understanding allows you to keep out of dangers. Seeking to do what Jesus wants, is so good God makes a promise to you. He offers a reward. You get to live a long life IF you are obedient to your parents.

Dear God,
Please help me to be a good listener to my parents. I know they love me, and want the best for me, even when I seem to want to do the thing I should not. Help me to see, that even when my parents say no to me, they want what is good and right for me. God, protect my parents and help their wisdom grow that I might continue to learn from them.

In Jesus Name, Amen.

DAY 9
PROVERBS 3:1-2 NIV

1 My son, do not forget my teaching, but keep my commands in your heart,

2 for they will prolong your life many years and bring you peace and prosperity.

Do you wish a long life? All God asks to give that promise to you, is that you obey the teachings of your parents. But obeying is not all. Think about this part of it. Keep HIS (the Lord's) commands in your heart. That means you do not just do because mommy and daddy say so. You store that command within the core of your being. You recognize and understand its importance. It's something you will never forget and likely will teach your own kids some day. Why, because it is in your heart.

For me this passage reminds me of how I never knew most of my grandparents, because of their love of alcohol. Their love was not Jesus. They did not store the good commands of the Lord in their heart. My parents taught us about Jesus. They taught us what a loving God is. They warned us about wrong things and encouraged us to do what is right. My mom still outlived her parents. My dad has outlived his dad by about 40 years! My dad is in his 80s.

Let's not forget the peace and prosperity that is also promised. God is so loving he promises us great things! Peace and prosperity are things adults long for. Prosperity is wealth. It's how much you have, not all about money. Wealth is measured in many ways.

A long life is a beautiful thing. You get to see your grandchildren, and maybe, just maybe your great grandchildren. Add in to this the incredible promise of peace and prosperity. Isn't it incredible that God gives us such a promise for simply obeying and storing HIS commands in our hearts?

Dear God,

Thank you for loving me so much that you offer me rewards for doing what is right. You are the only one who can keep these promises. You are the blessed one worthy of praise! Only a great and loving God can be so generous. Help me Lord to store your commands in my heart that I may not be easily led astray.

In Jesus Name, Amen.

DAY 10
PROVERBS 3: 3-4 (KJV)

3 Let not mercy and truth forsake you: bind them about your neck; write them upon the table of your heart:

4 So shalt you find favor and good understanding in the sight of God and man.

Mercy can be as simple as saying "I am sorry," or "I forgive you." Sometimes being forgiving can be hard. People can do things that make you real mad. But God showed his mercy to us in that while we were still sinners, Jesus died for us. Can we do any less?

Truth is easier to tell than a lie. A lie, you have to create, and then use. In addition to that you have to remember the lie you told. It gets even worse, to keep the lie you may have to tell more lies to paint your falsehood as true.

The following story was found in an 1860s textbook.

One day John returned to the bookstore. He asked to speak to the cashier. The cashier was purposefully ignoring him. The owner of the store walked up and asked what John wanted.

John handed the man a receipt and said, "I discovered I did not pay for this book when I got home."

The owner of the store looked at the date on the receipt. It was a week old. He asked John why it had taken so long to return. John explained he had to wait until his parents came back to the store. He handed the man the correct amount owed, including the exact amount for tax.

The man looked shocked. It was something for the boy to say he had not paid for the book, but then he was handing the man the money. He looked up the book, typed it into the register, and the bill was exactly what the young boy had handed him. "What is your name," he asked?

"John Masters."

"John when you are old enough to work, come find me and you can work here," the owner of the store said as he put the money in the cash drawer.

He then started to hand the boy a gift certificate for more books. But John said, "Sir, my parents taught me that doing what is right is its own reward. You showed me that by offering me a job when I get older.

In the story John does not hide a truth that will cost his wallet to be thinner. His honesty does turn out to be a reward. It earned him a favor in a future job. But even better, was knowing he did what was right. He didn't feel guilty anymore.

Dear God,

Help me to do what is right. Help me to not only tell the truth, but to make you proud of me when I do. For you know when I lie and when I fib. I want to be known for telling the truth.

Lord, please help me to be forgiving. Sometimes I get so mad I want to punch something. Sometimes I have to hold my breath, so I won't explode. God help me to do better. Help me to be forgiving. Help me to become a man of mercy.

In Jesus Name, Amen.

DAY 11
PROVERBS 3:5-6

5 Trust in the Lord with all your heart,
And lean not on your own understanding;

6 In all your ways acknowledge Him,
And He shall direct your paths.

The Lord is the most perfect person to trust! Why? Because He loves you and knows everything about you. Even things that other people don't know. He also knows everything else! There is not one question you could ask Him; that He couldn't answer! Another reason to trust Him is because He doesn't change His mind like we do. He never changes based on how He feels, like we do. He is solid as a rock! And you can always count on Him. Many people in the Bible trusted Him. He saw their faith in Him and He saved them. Many did not. They latter paid a heavy price. For not trusting and believing. If you trust the Lord with all your heart, He will never let you down!

Leaning on our own understanding is when we don't trust Him. When we fail to believe. We then do things our own way. But there is a price when we do that. We can get hurt doing this in many ways. Also, you can hurt other people, too. Like our family and friends; even strangers.

In all our ways, we should include God. Why? Because He will help us do what needs to be done. How do I know this? Because God has helped me with my job! When things got hard at times, I would ask for His help. Then I would get ideas in my mind on how to do a certain thing better. And it worked! Then I asked for more help. And more ideas came into my mind. I kept using them. Because they continued to work. Is there something you are having a hard time with? Trying to figure it out on your own? Include God. Ask Him to help you. He is always ready to do it!

Father,

Please help me to trust You more, because You don't lie and You can't either. Help me to include You in everything I do. Whether it's my schoolwork or my chores at home. Please show me how to do things better. So that those things I don't wish to do or do not like, may become easier.

In Jesus' name I pray and thank You. Amen.

DAY 12
PROVERBS 3:11-12

11 My son, do not despise the chastening of the Lord, do not detest His correction;

12 For whom the Lord loves He corrects, just as a father the son in whom He delights.

The father is telling his son here not to hate when we are punished by the Lord. At the time it will not feel good. It never does. Yet later we see why the punishment came. Also, why it was needed. As a rule, the Lord desires us to do good. Just like our parents do. Yet, often the Lord has to correct us and discipline us. Like our parents have to do as well to set us straight. To keep us from getting into more serious trouble. Both the Lord and our parents do this because they love us.

Please remember this when you happen to get into trouble. When you are punished for it ask God to forgive you for what you have done. Also apologize and ask your parents to forgive you. Then try not to repeat what has hurt them both.

As a boy, I was punished for something I did. The neighborhood kids were climbing a ladder placed against a very tall tree. They asked me if I would climb it. Without thinking, I climbed that tall ladder as fast as I could. When I reached a branch and sat on it, the ladder was knocked away from the tree! The children below were screaming with laughter. I was stuck and couldn't get down!

One of the children ran and told my mother (I'm glad my father was at work). She came out of the house screaming at me to get down from there. The kids put the ladder back and I climbed down. She then grabbed me and took me back in the house. We got to the back porch where she spanked me harder than I had ever been spanked before letting me go. Meanwhile the other kids saw everything! I was so embarrassed! That really hurt at the time. When I got older, I understood why she did what she did. It was because she loved me and she didn't want me to fall and get hurt or worse. When we are punished by the Lord or our parents, there is always a good reason behind it. Why? Because of how much they both love us.

Father God,
Please help me not to hate when I am punished. Help me to see where I was wrong. Remind me to ask for Your forgiveness when I'm wrong and help me to fix it.

In Jesus name I pray and thank You. Amen.

DAY 13
PROVERBS 3:9-10

9 Honor the Lord with your possessions,
And with the first fruits of all your increase;

10 So your barns will be filled with plenty,
And your vats will overflow with new wine.

Psalm 24:1 says, "The earth is the Lord's and all its fullness, the world and those who dwell therein." This means everything belongs to God. Why? Because He made the place where we live. He helps the food to grow that we eat. These things and others He blessed us with to enjoy. We should always be grateful and thankful for that. That is honoring the Lord with what we have. Reminding ourselves that these things come from Him. This should bring great respect to Him. Also, what He gives us we can give back to Him by way of the tithe. Ten percent of what money we may receive from working, and even your allowance, is your tithe. If you put this and keep this into practice, more can come your way. You can have more than enough. You can also have enough to share.

I was not always good at this. Before now, bills kept coming. And my paycheck seemed to get smaller and smaller. Why? Because I used what I was supposed to give to God on something else. Money ran out faster than I was making it. Then I decided to tithe again. I prayed that the Lord would help me get out of this hole I was in. And He did. By going back to the right thing, tithing, I actually began to have extra! That is always a good thing. Begin to give back to God. Be faithful with it and see what He will do!

Dear Father,

Please help me to remember everything I have, came from You. It also belongs to You. Help me to honor You with what You give me. By giving some of it back. Please use it to bless someone else. As much as You have blessed me.

In Jesus name I pray and thank You. Amen.

DAY 14
PROVERBS 3:13-14

13 Happy is the man who finds wisdom, and the man who gains understanding;

14 For her proceeds are better than the profits of silver, and her gain more than fine gold.

———————————————————————

Ever finally learn something that you really wanted to know? How did it make you feel? Happy, right?

That's exactly what wisdom does when you find it. It's not only like a light bulb going on in your head.

It is also light going into your heart. Wisdom keeps us safe. Wisdom helps us to have peace also. This is why it is more valuable than gold or silver. You really can't put a price on it either. It is that precious and that important. Aren't you also glad when you understand something? That happened to me a lot in school growing up. The more I understood something, the more I wanted to know about it. Is that the same with you? Especially if it's something you really like!

This can also apply to your knowledge of God. The more you know about Him, the more you would want to know. He wants you to know Him. Try to find out more about Him and see how happy you can become.

———————————————————————

Dear Father,

Please help me to find wisdom. Please help me to understand You more. Please give me Your wisdom so I can live the right way. Help me to know the happiness that comes from knowing You. And from finding wisdom.

I pray and thank You in Jesus name. Amen

DAY 15
PROVERBS 3:15-18

15 She is more precious than rubies, and all the things you may desire cannot compare with her.

16 Length of days is in her right hand, in her left hand riches and honor.

17 Her ways are ways of pleasantness, and all her paths are peace.

18 She is a tree of life to those who take hold of her, and happy are all who retain her.

The writer here is speaking of wisdom as a woman. I have yet to find out why. I'm just guessing here, but maybe because of how loving and sweet she can be. If you had a gazillion of something you always wanted, that can't beat wisdom. Wisdom is good on its own. Yet there are other benefits with having it. Your life here on earth can be extended, if you use wisdom the right way. If you really think things through. Also asking questions about things you don't know yet. That's how you can get even more wisdom. Not just from the Bible, which is the best book for it. Older people you know and trust can give you wisdom, too. Always ask God for wisdom also. He is always ready to share it at any time we ask Him. Lastly, when we follow wisdom, we are ready to enjoy the life and peace that it gives! So, grab hold of wisdom and hold it tight!

Dear Father,
Help me to call on You on things I don't understand. Remind me
to ask my parents and my teachers, too. Please help me to keep
the wisdom and knowledge I receive from Your Word and from
others.

In Jesus name I pray and thank You. Amen.

DAY 16
PROVERBS 3:19-20

19 The Lord by wisdom founded the earth; by understanding He established the heavens;

20 By His knowledge the depths were broken up, and clouds drop down the dew.

This part of the chapter gives us a little taste of how great and awesome God is! With the enormous amount of what God knows, He made everything we see. Even the things we cannot see. Things that are too small for the human eye! God made the earth by what? By wisdom! Why? Because things had to be done in a certain way. To get what we have and enjoy. The land has to be high enough, so the oceans don't wash it away. If that happened, we would have no place to live! The oceans are broken up by the land we live on. Who could stay on a big ball of water! He knew we needed a place to put our feet. A place also to grow our food. To have the many animals we like. And some we may not like, because they can be dangerous! I hope you don't run into any of those! God built where He lives. With thousands upon thousands of angels and creatures worshipping Him. Praising His name to be heard from one end of the universe to the other! That's how great God is and much, much more!

Dear Father,
Let me see the beauty of all You have made. It is so wonderful and interesting. Even too big for my mind sometimes. Please help me to appreciate all You have made and to thank You for it also.

In Jesus name I pray and thank You. Amen.

DAY 17
PROVERBS 3:21-24

21 My son, let not them depart from your eyes--Keep sound wisdom and discretion;

22 So they will be life to your soul And grace to your neck.

23 Then you will walk safely in your way, And your foot will not stumble.

24 When you lie down, you will not be afraid; Yes, you will lie down and your sleep will be sweet.

———————————————

Boys, don't let wisdom out of your sight! It is very important to life! It is important on how to live as well. You are also to keep wisdom close. Discretion means to be careful of how you do things and of how you treat other people, too. There is a good blessing when you are careful. You have less of a chance of hurting others, or getting hurt yourself. That's a good thing. Always! The benefit of keeping wisdom is that you can enjoy peace. Enough to rest in when night comes. You can always sleep well, knowing you have done right. Another benefit is being safe where you go. Because you think about what to do ahead of time. This is also discretion. Be careful how we act.

———————————————

Dear Father,

Please help me to keep wisdom, with all the other things I learn from You, my parents; and my teachers. Help me to walk safely by living what You and they tell me.

I pray and thank You in Jesus name. Amen.

DAY 18
PROVERBS 3:25-26

25 Do not be afraid of sudden terror, Nor of trouble from the wicked when it comes;

26 For the Lord will be your confidence, And will keep your foot from being caught.

No one, absolutely no one can protect us like the Lord! How do I know? From experience! I can brag on God all day! One day in particular was Christmas Eve of last year. I was shopping for dinner at a supermarket. When I was done, I loaded my car with my food. Then I started to go home. But I didn't make it. Not then anyways. As I was coming out into the street, I was hit by a truck. It was bad! My left headlight was crushed. The hood of my car was bent upward. And my license plate was knocked off to the sidewalk.

The person that hit me ran a red light! He should have stopped but he didn't. Where was God in all this?

The only damage that was suffered was by the car only! I was not touched on impact. Thank God for that! The truck only hit the front end of the car. Had he hit the door, it could have been a lot worse! You can always trust God to protect you! He has for me! When bad people come our way, God has something for them, too. We may not get to see it. Yet, He works on our behalf! Always. Because He's always looking out for us!

Dear Father,

I am grateful and thankful that You protect me. Thank You for protecting my family and friends, too.

In Jesus name I pray and thank You. Amen.

DAY 19
PROVERBS 3:27-28

27 Do not withhold good from those to whom it is due, When it is in the power of your hand to do so.

28 Do not say to your neighbor, "Go and come back, and tomorrow I will give it," When you have it with you.

How many of us have done this? Unfortunately, I have. I also regretted it afterwards, too. When the other person left. Yet I did have the chance to make it right. For that I was glad! This means we shouldn't hold back anything we owe someone. Especially, when we are able to pay that person. Sometimes other things come to mind to spend it on. You and I still need to do the right thing. We don't know how badly the other person needs it. Don't we expect to get what someone owes us? We are to give others that same respect! At the moment when asked, please give it, and make God smile!

Dear Father,

Help me to pay what I owe when I owe. Don't let me put this off anymore. I want You to smile at me. When you see me do the right thing and pay.

In Jesus name I pray and thank You. Amen.

DAY 20
PROVERBS 3:29-30

29 Do not devise evil against your neighbor, For he dwells by you for safety's sake.

30 Do not strive with a man without cause, If he has done you no harm.

Have you ever heard of the expression "no brainer"? This means some things require no thinking. What has been said is as plain as day. You can't miss its meaning. I love verses like that! Straight to the point. Life has enough bad things to deal with. Living by these words can keep those things down. They won't happen as often either. If you plan something bad for someone, that's not good. On the other hand, by you being good bait, people are safe around you. They can trust you and they may ask you to pray for them. Be ready because you never know.

Also, if there's nothing wrong, don't make up something just to argue. That's not good either. Especially when you have no reason to. The Bible says "as far as it depends on you, live in peace with all men". Meaning be aware of how you treat those around you. And say you're sorry when you have to.

Father,

Please help me to treat people the way I want to be treated. Help me not to argue for no reason. Please help me to pray if someone asks me to.

I pray and thank You in Jesus name. Amen

DAY 21
PROVERBS 3:31-32

31 Do not envy the oppressor, And choose none of his ways;

32 For the perverse person is an abomination to the Lord, But His secret counsel is with the upright.

No one should want to be like a mean king or ruler, or a mean judge. With the power they have, they can do a lot of good. Oppressors are nasty and selfish! They only look out for themselves! Their ways are evil in the sight of God. He sees everything they do! He sees what we do, too! Abomination is heard a lot in the Bible. That means this is something God really hates!

God tells His secrets to good people - to people who are trying hard to live right. I think some of those secrets help them do just that. This shows others as well as us how to get it right. The Bible is filled with good examples. Of people hearing from God and doing what He said. The outcome is always right. While sometimes it can be painful. Nevertheless, when God shares something it is ultimately for our good! We can trust Him for that!

Dear Father,

Please help me not to be mean and rude to people just to get my own way. Help me to think of others first before myself. Like Your Son Jesus did. When He gave His life for me.

In His name I pray and thank You. Amen.

DAY 22
PROVERBS 3:34

34 Surely He scorns the scornful, But gives grace to the humble.

In a show of hands, how many of us need grace?! We all do! The humble receives grace from God. They realize that they need His help. The humble are always ready to hear His wisdom to do things right and even better without having to do it twice. I remember growing up doing just that...doing something twice that my mother had told me to do. I was tired of working. All I wanted to do was to go outside and play: play kickball, foot races or climbing trees. But we won't go there! Lol! When you think you know it all, you find out quickly you don't! If you have an attitude with God, or even with your parents, they will put you in check!

Quick!

Learn to be humble. Why? That will get you farther ahead than an attitude! And grace is a bonus when God sees we want to do what is right.

Father,

Please show me how to be humble. So that I may receive Your grace whenever I may need it.

In Jesus name I pray and thank You. Amen

DAY 23
PROVERBS 3:35

35 The wise shall inherit glory, But shame shall be the legacy of fools.

Being wise has a lot of benefits. It keeps us safe. It keeps us out of trouble. We also can receive glory from it too. Honor and respect can come with it - not to mention a good name. Live to be wise, so you may enjoy these things. If you don't, the opposite can happen...you will be remembered as being foolish. There is no fun in that! Shame is very hard to get rid of, it lingers. That's not good when you remember when you messed up. Live to be wise so this doesn't happen.

Father,

Help me to be wise. Please help me to live in Your wisdom. Help me to learn Your ways. Let me have a good name.

In Jesus name I pray and thank You. Amen

DAY 24
PROVERBS 4: 1-2

1 Hear, you children, the instruction of a father, and attend to know understanding.

2 For I give you good doctrine, forsake ye not my law. For I was my father's son, tender and only [beloved] in the sight of my mother.

Do you remember your parents saying things like, "When I was your age...," "I wish I had It easy as you do...." Yes, as hard as it is to believe they were once young kids also. That means your father and mother have done many of the foolish things you have done and will do. It means they do not wish for you to make the same mistakes, because they learned from those things and sometimes mistakes have heavy penalties.

While mistakes are often learning tools, isn't it better to have someone to guide you? In a video game with hidden treasures you need to win, isn't it better when you know someone who has beaten a level? They can tell you how to win! That is no different than what your parents are doing when they say no to you. They are helping you win a level of life.

Oh, make no mistake, parents want the best for you. They want you to have a better life than they had. That's why they work so hard!

Will you store away what your father and mother teach about you God? Will you remember the rules for living even when you are as old as they are? Store those things away in your heart and mind. Keep them - they are precious gold.

I hope you are not laughing yet, and thinking, "how can my mom and dad saying no to me be precious gold?" Well, it may sound ridiculous now, but when you grow older you suddenly understand all those noes and yeses. If you store these things in your heart and mind, when you grow older you will find yourself laughing when you have your own kids. Why? Because you will start to say yes or no and remember being the one to whom that was said for whatever reason it was being said.

Dear God!

Help me to store away what my mom and dad teach me. Help me to think on what they say whether it is no or yes and see their wisdom as your hand guiding them.

Lord, I am still growing. I still do a lot of things I know I should not do. Help me to seek your Word. Help me to desire to do what is right more than I do what is wrong.

Please remind me my parents were kids once too, so I may seek their wisdom just as I do others to learn how to beat a game. God protect my parents. Keep them safe so I may continue to learn and grow in their love.

In Jesus Name, Amen.

DAY 25
PROVERBS 4:5-9

5 Get wisdom, get understanding: forget [it] not; neither decline from the words of my mouth.

6 Forsake her not, and she shall preserve you: love her, and she shall keep you.

7 Wisdom [is] the principal thing; [therefore] get wisdom: and with all your getting get understanding.

8 Exalt her, and she shall promote you: she shall bring you to honor, when you do embrace her.

9 She shall give to your head an ornament of grace: a crown of glory shall she deliver to you.

What are you doing to get wisdom and understanding? Are

you doing your best in school? Are you reading at home? Are you asking questions when you do not know the answers? Are you studying?

A principal thing is a thing we should put first. Our faith in Jesus always comes first, Family always comes second and country third. But, what does it mean to make wisdom important, or rather the getting of wisdom and understanding? What would that look like if we follow King Solomon's advice here?

Wouldn't this mean we should be thinking about what can we learn next? Play is also important. Fun is important. But gaining wisdom and understanding---. Play is for the moment. It's fun and then it is over. Wisdom – it's hard work getting wisdom and understanding. But when you are done. when you learn that new thing, NO ONE CAN TAKE THAT FROM YOU!

When I was young, we had a lot of games to play. One of them was like a football game. One guy had a ball. Everyone jumped him to get the ball. The guy who got the ball became the next target. It was rough and fun play. When the game was over, depending on the rules the boys playing had set, the boy who had the ball longest could walk home with the ball.

When you learn something, NO ONE can take that. Its stored in your brain. The cool thing about a brain is it is like a bottomless box. There always seems to be room for more to learn. What are you filling it with?

If you work hard in school, and fight to learn, that knowledge can be like a crown. After High School, there are colleges and real life on the job opportunities to learn. The one who works hard to get wisdom and understanding can become wealthy in many ways. No one knows that better than Solomon. He was a King with great wealth.

Dear God,

Help me. I need your help to like learning. Help me to get what is hard for me. I hate learning about_____. Lord, give me the ability to get this into my head. Help me to learn these things. Help me to see the importance in becoming a better learner.

Jesus, help me to see the rewards ahead for learning.

In Jesus name, Amen.

DAY 26
PROVERBS 4:10-12 NIV

10 Listen, my son, accept what I say, and the years of your life will be many.

11 I instruct you in the way of wisdom and lead you along straight paths.

12 When you walk, your steps will not be hampered; when you run, you will not stumble.

Listening to parents and being obedient is a command. God's reward to you is that you will live a long life. Think about learning God's Word like this: There once was a boy named Boomer. Boomer was just a jerk who didn't ever do what he was asked. He would talk back to his parents, and he would try things just because he heard his mom say no to them once. He was not the kind of kid you bring home to share with your parents.

Then one day, one of Boomer's friends introduced him to Jesus. Boomer was curious about this God who loved. Then he decided, I have to try. He committed his life to Jesus!

Boomer began to read the Bible every day. Suddenly, he started to change.

The kid he used to put in the garbage pail when he passed by, shrunk smaller as Boomer got closer, trying to hide when Boomer passed by him. Boomer remembered how it made him happy to put that kid in the garbage can. He had done it so many times, that after he accepted Christ, he continued until one day he read in the Bible, "'Honor your father and [your] mother,' and, 'You shall love your neighbor as yourself.' '" (Mat 19:19 NKJV). He suddenly realized that putting the kid in the garbage can was not the sort of thing he should be doing, because it wasn't something he would want done to himself.

You could say the Bible shone a light on something that made Boomer stumble (sin). He never again treated the smaller boy like he did before. All of a sudden Boomer started to treat him like his own brother.

Dear God,

Help me to store your wisdom and my parent's wisdom within me. Help me to see how your wisdom can lead me to live a long life.

Lord, help me. You know where I sin and am tempted to do wrong again and again. I ask Lord that you change me and make me better. Help me to become the bait that draws others to you. Help me to be your shining light on a hill.

In Jesus name, Amen.

DAY 27
PROVERBS 4:13-19

13 Take fast hold of instruction; let [her] not go: keep her; for she [is] your life.

14 Enter not into the path of the wicked and go not in the way of evil [men].

15 Avoid it, pass not by it, turn from it, and pass away.

16 For they sleep not, except they have done mischief; and their sleep is taken away, unless they cause [some] to fall.

17 For they eat the bread of wickedness and drink the wine of violence.

18 But the path of the just [is] as the shining light, that shines more and more unto the perfect day.

19 The way of the wicked [is] as darkness: they know not at what they stumble.

Have you caught that King Solomon, the author of this book in the Bible, seems to be repeating himself a lot about the importance of learning? When something is important it gets repeated, just like when you are learning to do something new in math, or when you are learning to spell something hard. Repetition should tell you that something is very important to the person who is teaching it.

So, King Solomon talks again about instruction. This time the push is not on getting it, but it is on keeping it. I learned to read Braille in the '90s to work with a blind student. Braille is a special code for the Blind to write and read in. But, because I no longer use that knowledge, it has become rusty. I can't think of how to write things in Braille anymore. I can still read it and get little refreshers when I read signs on walls, like the ones by elevators. But unless I start using that knowledge a lot, it fades.

There are TV shows that talk about how your knowledge can save you. There are a few shows that have men surviving in extreme weather. What they were taught about survival becomes alert in their minds and keeps them safe.

What you learn from the Bible can keep you safe also. Imagine, having a ton of choices, and only one of them is right. Only one choice can be the right one.

(As far as we know, photo is public domain)

How do you choose what to do? What would help you choose what to do? In life, what you learn from the Bible can help guide you. That is why one of the nicknames for the Bible is "Passport."

Now a simple question to consider, "If you are reading the Bible every day, are you likely to go in the way of evil men?"

My bet is you will easily avoid those evil men. Bet you never thought about how hard it is for them to sleep if they don't do something bad. It's like they have to do something sinful to feel at ease enough to fall asleep.

That may sound scary. It should! After all, their lives evolve around being lazy, skipping school, breaking the law, being disrespectful, cussing, and so much more that is wrong.

The sad thing here is that they do not even know that when they make bad choices, they are causing themselves to stumble.

Dear God,

Thank you for giving me your Word, the Bible, to direct my paths and teach me about you. Help me to keep in my heart and mind what I learn from it.

God help me to choose not to be a follower of boys that make wrong choices. Help me to follow You, even if that means standing alone. It is more important that I do what you want, then what I want. You're far smarter than I am!

God, please guide my footsteps, help me to make good choices. I know I do a lot of stupid things. Help me to choose better. Help me to think of you first so I can do the wise things.

In Jesus name, Amen.

DAY 28
PROVERBS 4:20-23

20 My son, attend to my words; incline thine ear unto my sayings.

21 Let them not depart from thine eyes; keep them in the midst of thine heart.

22 For they [are] life unto those that find them, and health to all their flesh.

23 Keep thy heart with all diligence; for out of it [are] the issues of life.

By now you are probably asking how many times is King Solomon going to talk about being a good listener, and the importance of listening to your parents. Well, you may be surprised to learn there is a reason things are repeated.

Children and adults both make mistakes. But boys as I have said, do the stupid things. We do the things, we know are wrong, sometimes just to see what will happen no matter how many times we have been told not to do something. In some ways it is funny how many times we must pound something into our heads, before it sticks.

I know this is a story about boys, but this passage reminds me of a story about a cute little girl named Amanda. Amanda was 7 years old. She lived with her mom and dad who lived just behind a few small rolling hills. These hills were perfect for rolling down. You know what I am talking about: short hills that make you think about laying down and rolling down the hill. Amanda loved doing this. Her parents warned her not to do this by the house. There were some pipes sticking out of the ground close by. Her mom and dad said this to her a few times every day it seemed. "Go roll over there Not here." "See this pipe. You could get hurt if you hit it, go role over there."

Yes, you guessed it, one day Amanda rolled down that hill smack dab into that pipe! SCREEECH! Amanda screamed. She went from being a cute beautiful little girl to being a scary mess that made her father feel faint. She was rushed to the hospital. Amanda got about 8 stitches right in the middle of her forehead.

Do you think Amanda rolled down that hill again?

All of a sudden, the warnings her parents gave her about the pipe were written inside her heart.

Dear God,

I know when your Word tells me something and seems to repeat the message over and over, there is something I must learn. No matter how many times I try to ignore it.

Help me God. I need to put those warnings from my parents, those little lessons, those important things they want me to learn, in my heart so I may never forget them.

Lord Jesus, you gave me wonderful parents to watch over me. Keep them safe. Guide them as you are guiding me, so I may continue to grow in you more each day.

In your Name, Amen!

DAY 29
PROVERBS 4:24-25

24 Put away from you a deceitful mouth, And put perverse lips far from you.

25 Let your eyes look straight ahead, And your eyelids look right before you.

It's nice to know that God knows where we are in our lives. He knows when we lie. He knows when we cuss, even if the lies and cusses are only in our thoughts.

But here, God wants us to think before we say something. I don't know if you understand how hard that is sometimes. Sometimes it's like the mouth has a direct line to the brain and simply says what we are thinking out loud. That can be embarrassing. Sometimes we simply say things we wish we never did.

When you are young, this is the best time to begin to tame that tongue. It's time to begin to choose to be different than those you know who cuss and lie all the time. You can create a whole new you from simply doing these things. instead of pouting and spouting when you get mad. Zipping the lip, holding your tongue and remembering King Solomon, the wisest King ever, advised his son to put away such things.

Verse 25 is slightly different. "Let your eyes look straight ahead." In the NIV it says, "and your gaze be right before you."

If you have to follow a path, when there are a lot of little trails that curve off and disappear, it's not easy to always be looking ahead and keeping your eyes on the prize. Which of course, is the end of the path. If you're like me, I look to see where these little paths go and think about what it might be like to go there. In life, when you want something, you learn the Importance of focusing.

When you want to become a better runner, you practice running every day. You run a mile, then you run two or three miles. You think about winning races. Where is your gaze? Is it on the prize then? The end of the race! YES!

What will it mean for you to win the race of life and be embraced by Jesus at the end of your days when you are old? Think on that prize. Is setting a guard over our mouths a small thing then? YES! Is the prize worth it? YES!

Dear God,

Help me to think before I speak. Help me to choose words that help, not hurt. Even when I only want to such things to myself, Lord help me choose better words. Let me be known as someone who loves you.

Jesus, please help me to keep my eyes on you. Help me to think of what you desire for my life. Help me to focus and keep my eyes on your prize!

I want to be like you. Help me to seek your glory by being an example to others of how great you are to me. Make me the bait that draws others to you.

In Jesus Name, Amen.

DAY 30
PROVERBS 4:26-27

26 Ponder the path of thy feet and let all thy ways be established.

27 Turn not to the right hand nor to the left: remove thy foot from evil.

Consider that Jeremiah 10:23 states "O LORD, I know that the way of man [is] not in himself: [it is] not in man that walks to direct his steps." Think about this. Can you choose where you walk? Can you choose where you go? ABSOLUTELY! So how does the above passage and Jeremiah 10:23 mesh. How do they make sense?

Well, have you ever been told its important to think before you speak? Have you ever been asked after you did something stupid, "You didn't use your brain did you?" Oh, I am sure your Mom or Dad has something they say when they know you didn't think something through. Proverbs here tells us to think before we act. It tells us to keep on the path God set out for us.

The passage in Jeremiah adds something to thinking. It tells us that we choose the wrong thing because the devil is out there waving something attractive before us, like a yummy Snickers Bar right after school, if we do something—something we should not do. We do not choose to do wrong, because it is wrong, we choose the wrong thing because it is attractive to us.

God tries to remind us, that His way is better. He does this by keeping His promises and so many other things it's amazing we do not easily follow Him all the time. But just as we want to be fishers of men, there are evil spirits out there doing what the devil wants by tempting us to do things God does not want us to do. So, they are trying to use things they know we like to get us off the path of following Jesus.

We must follow Jesus. We must take the path He shows us. Jesus never promises us an easy life. But he promises us an ETERNAL reward. He promises so much more and long lasting than those things the devil wishes for us to do.

Dear Lord Jesus,

Help me to think before I act. Help me to think before I speak. Help me to think on You!

I know I often do things I should not. Please help me to take a quick breath and ask, "What would Jesus do?"

Lord God, I want what you desire for me. I want to do what is right in your eyes for me. For I know your rewards are greater than any others!

Thank you, Jesus for your promises!

In Jesus Name, Amen.

DAY 31
PROVERBS 5:1-2

1 My son, pay attention to my wisdom; Lend your ear to my understanding,

2 That you may preserve discretion, And your lips may keep knowledge.

The young should always pay attention to those who are older. Reason being they have more experience in life than you. For where you are going, they have already been. They have also made mistakes that they would not want you to make. Mistakes are often painful. Some can and will be remembered for a long time. Giving your ear to understanding may prevent this. If you have understanding, You can know the outcome of what you do and say. Keeping discretion means to think before you act...or even speak. Without it, the wrong thing is easily done. And we don't want that, do we?

Father,
Please help me to listen to those older than me. Give me ears to listen and understand. Help me to hear what is right and to do it. Help me to think before doing something. Even before speaking. Help me always to keep wisdom and to use it.

In Jesus name I pray and thank You. Amen.

DAY 32
PROVERBS 5:12-14

12 And say: "How I have hated instruction, And my heart despised correction!

13 I have not obeyed the voice of my teachers, Nor inclined my ear to those who instructed me!

14 I was on the verge of total ruin, In the midst of the assembly and congregation."

The verses before these talk about a mistake the son had made. But what he says afterwards tells you the pain he's feeling for not listening to those who tried to teach him. For not listening to those who were trying to help him avoid the mistake he made. It is always important to listen. When you don't understand something, always ask questions. Asking questions is a great way of learning and understanding. By not listening, the son nearly lost all he had. Not only that, everyone around him knew about his mistake! This is a terrible thing -- to not do the right thing and then pay for it -- With everyone watching! That is so embarrassing!

By all means, please keep yourselves from this! No one should live in shame or embarrassment.

Father,

Please help me to receive, willingly receive, instruction. To embrace it and to use it. So, I can make as few mistakes as possible. Help me not to do embarrassing things. Keep me from the things that bring pain and shame.

I pray and thank You in Jesus name. Amen.

DAY 33
PROVERBS 5:21-23

21 For the ways of man are before the eyes of the Lord, And He ponders all his paths.

22 His own iniquities entrap the wicked man, And he is caught in the cords of his sin.

23 He shall die for lack of instruction, And in the greatest of his folly he shall go astray

The Lord sees everything we do. He watches also everywhere we go! How do I know? Because I have lived it! Before coming back to church, I was deep in trouble. Trouble with sin. I did whatever made me feel good. This is not a good thing. Why? Because you can easily become trapped in it iwthout seeing any way out! You can't see any way to get away from it. Like the verse says, you can feel tied up, and that's no way to live. I'm still learning not to live that way...even at my age! That's one great thing about life. You never get too old to learn! Yet, if you fall down, get back up! Don't stay in the mistake you may have made. Get up and keep moving forward!

Father,

Please remind me that You watch me every day and see everything I do. Help me to do what is right in Your eyes. Help me to stay away from sin. Help me to learn from my mistakes and to keep moving forward.

I pray and thank You in Jesus name. Amen.

DAY 34
PROVERBS 6:1-5

1 My son, if you have put up security for your neighbor, have given your pledge for a stranger,

2 if you are snared in the words of your mouth, caught in the words of your mouth,

3 then do this, my son, and save yourself, for you have come into the hand of your neighbor: go, hasten, and plead urgently with your neighbor.

4 Give your eyes no sleep and your eyelids no slumber;

5 save yourself like a gazelle from the hand of the hunter, like a bird from the hand of the fowler.

When I first read this passage I had to think, and asked myself, "what are they talking about?" Asking questions is how we learn after all.

The security they are talking about is a promise, that you will pay if your neighbor does not. I suddenly, totally understood this. After all that is one of the stupid things I have done and paid the penalty for my lack of my wisdom.

As a young man, I had a friend who needed to buy a car. He was a great friend. We did things together every day. In order for him to get the car, I had to promise to make payments, if he did not. I thought sure, it's not something I should ever worry about happening.

One day I was walking around wondering why my friend was not where I always saw him. Then someone told me, he had moved. So, I went to see if this was true. His place was empty. Nothing left in it!

OK, I thought maybe something happened where he got called away for some reason. I tried calling him. His phone was disconnected. It was then that I got scared. Suddenly, it hit me that I could end up paying for his car!

A month later, I was making payments on his car. A car I did not have. A car that my "friend," still had. Yes, somewhere he was probably using it to go wherever he wanted.

As you can see it was foolishness for me to guarantee his ability to pay for the car. I ended up paying for something I did not use. Do you see how I was caught in the snare of my own words? Do you see how if I had listened to the wisdom of this passage, I would have kept that money in my pocket?

When you make a stupid mistake like this, you do lose sleep. You wish you could run away and hide your head because you feel stupid and used.

Oh, I did find that "friend." I did plead with him. I learned how easily I was snared by my own words. He did not care how this affected me. He did not care that I was paying for something he used. As a result, I told where his car was and had it repossessed.

That made me smile, but I was still stuck with paying for the car after it was resold for however much was still owed. Some lessons of life hurt. This one did. On top of that, I was angry at the world for my own stupidity. Worse, it became hard to forgive my friend for the evil he did sticking me with his bill.

Dear Lord,

Help me God, not to do stupid things. Help me to follow your wisdom. Help me to seek to do what is right in your eyes.

Lord, let me follow your will. Let me seek to please you first. Help me to forgive, even when it is hard.

In Jesus Name, Amen.

DAY 35
PROVERBS 6:6-11

6 Go to the ant, thou sluggard; consider her ways, and be wise:

7 Which having no guide, overseer, or ruler,

8 Provides her meat in the summer, [and] gathers her food in the harvest.

9 How long wilt you sleep, O sluggard? when will you arise out of your sleep?

10 [Yet] a little sleep, a little slumber, a little folding of the hands to sleep:

11 So shall your poverty come as one that travels, and your want as an armed man

When I was thinking about this it just hit me how much knowledge of science and life King Solomon had. He knew there was no queen for the ants like there is for bees.

Dr. Deborah Gordon gave a talk in 2015 talking about the ants not having a leader. She said the world's largest colony stretched 3,700 miles. We all know how small ants are. Imagine having to feed all of them! Yet, the ant knows to gather food for the winter and is always working to provide for the colony.

Sluggards are lazy people. They complain about getting up and beg to sleep in all the time. They detest chores. They promise to do them tomorrow, but that tomorrow never becomes today.

Sluggards are ok with you doing work and providing for them. But have a problem when it is their turn to do the work.

Aesop who lived about 500 years before Jesus wrote a story on this.

The Ants & the Grasshopper

One bright day in late autumn a family of Ants were bustling about in the warm sunshine, drying out the grain they had stored up during the summer, when a starving Grasshopper, his fiddle under his arm, came up and humbly begged for a bite to eat.

"What!" cried the Ants in surprise, "haven't you stored anything away for the winter? What in the world were you doing all last summer?"

"I didn't have time to store up any food," whined the Grasshopper; "I was so busy making music that before I knew it the summer was gone."

The Ants shrugged their shoulders in disgust.

"Making music, were you?" they cried. "Very well; now dance!" And they turned their backs on the Grasshopper and went on with their work.

The moral of the story is: there's a time for work and a time for play.

Dear God,

Help me not be lazy, keep me from being like the sluggard. I want to be the one who stores things away to be ready in a time of need. God, I want to be wise. I want to be the one who is prepared because I listened to you.

Lord, please help me to do my chores even when I do not want to. Help me not to complain, because your word tells us work is a good thing. Lord, also help me to remember there is a time for play and a time for work. Give me the wisdom to know the difference

In Jesus Name, Amen.

DAY 36
PROVERBS 6:12-15

12 A troublemaker and a villain, who goes about with a corrupt mouth,

13 who winks maliciously with his eye, signals with his feet and motions with his fingers,

14 who plots evil with deceit in his heart--he always stirs up conflict.

15 Therefore disaster will overtake him in an instant; he will suddenly be destroyed--without remedy.

Troublemakers always seem to know what to say to make people mad. I had a classmate named Michael who had curly red hair and was the tallest kid in the classroom. Michael would say and do things that just seemed to be wrong in so many ways. He was also a bully. Michael had his followers. They would copy every little thing he did.

My friend Donald and I were different. We stood up for each other. We tried to honor our parents by doing what was right. Michael, well, we thought he did well getting himself sent to the principal's office. That was what we viewed with fear. You see back then the principal had a paddle and he used it. So, your bottom got a reminder of the expectation to behave. To us that was being "suddenly destroyed."

In the adult world, the closest comparison I can think of is how the drug dealer lives, and how short the lives are of drug dealers. Many die young or go to jail.

But we have hope in Jesus. We have parents and teachers who set us on the right path. Don't they deserve our thanks? They do everything they can to show us what is right and good and just. We owe them a thank you for setting us on that right path.

Dear God,

Help me NOT to do foolish and wicked things. Keep my heart set on you, so that what I say and do may shine a light on who You are to those around me.

Lord, I pray for my parents. Bless them for taking care of me. Bless them for setting my feet on the right path. Lord, help me to be as good as they are that I may be the bait for others to follow Jesus.

In Jesus Name, Amen.

DAY 37
PROVERBS 6:16-19

16 These six [things] does the LORD hate: yea, seven [are] an abomination unto him:

17 A proud look, a lying tongue, and hands that shed innocent blood,

18 A heart that devises wicked imaginations, feet that are swift in running to mischief,

19 A false witness [that] speaks lies, and he that sows discord among brethren.

Sin is something the Lord hates. Sin is what separates us from God.

1. "A proud look" comes from having pride in yourself. Pride is what puffed up the devil and made him think he could be equal with God. There is a saying that pride goes before a fall. It is a hard life lesson if you are the one to learn it.

2. "A lying tongue"—this sin can do a world of damage bigger than you can imagine. God wants us as Christians to be seen as trustworthy, to be seen as the persons that people seek out because they believe in us.

3. "Hands that shed innocent blood" – this is a reference to murder, to taking the life of another.

4. "A heart that devises wicked imaginations" – You may actually know someone who seems to be that person who is always coming up with ideas, and so many of them lead into trouble. In many ways this passage is talking about the leaders of those who get into trouble.

5. "Feet that are swift in running to mischief" – the followers, who seek to join in wherever trouble and mischief are found. So not only are the leaders in trouble with God, but all those who would also do sinful things because they followed someone else.

6. "A false witness that speaks lies" – If you ever needed someone to stand up and bail you out with an excuse or witnessed something and saw you were not to blame, you know how it could have went if that person lied. I once worked with someone who did this. She said she saw something and lied about it. Her lies became so bad, every time she talked to me, I wanted a witness. Her lies were so bad, that she was often caught in them. Some cost her boss money.

7. "He that sows discord among brethren" – Discord is like division. When a person creates this he/she says or does something that puts a wall between your friend(s) and you. I have met a few people who actually go from place to place doing this. They create what we call infighting, then sit back and watch. These people like to sit back and smile as they watch what their words have created.

Lord Jesus,

Help me to pursue after you and your wisdom. Help me to choose to do sinful things. Help me to choose the things that bring me closer to you.

Lord, help me to pray for those who have committed one of these 7 things against me. Help me to pray for them that they also may know your love.

In Jesus name, Amen.

DAY 38
PROVERBS 6:20-22

20 My son, keep your father's commandment, and forsake not the law of your mother:

21 Bind them continually upon your heart, [and] tie them about your neck.

22 When you go, it shall lead you; when you sleep, it shall keep you; and [when] you awake, it shall talk with you.

When you are obedient to your father and mother, there are good things that happen. Right now, the choices you make on whether to obey or not create lifelong behaviors. Yes, your choice to behave, your choice to listen to your mom and dad, your choice to not do something and your choice to do something will affect you when you are older.

Surprised? I think if someone told me this at your age, I might have laughed at them. I don't think I would have meant to be rude. It would be that I couldn't understand how my choice to do as my mom and dad wanted by looking both ways before I cross the street could affect my whole life.

Now, I bet I have your attention. You see at the age of 6, I was allowed to cross two streets to go visit friends on my own. Life was simpler then. It was a safer world. Today this is not always possible because the world is much more dangerous. But back to crossing the street. If I chose not to look both ways (Even though my Mom walked me across those two streets until she was sure I would do it on my own, then watched me to make sure I did it on my own, before she trusted me.), is it possible my life would be much different today? Do you think I may be walking with a bigger limp today? Maybe I might not be around?

Parents teach us many things to protect and keep us throughout life. Our choices to keep what they say in our hearts can make us successful in the future. I look back on life now that I am old enough to be a grandfather and think about some of the things my mom taught me and smile. Here are a few of the things I learned:

1. Respect your elders.
2. Trust your heart. If something feels wrong don't do it!
3. Girls have to be treated specially. Open the door for them.
4. Stealing is wrong.
5. Lying is wrong.
6. Stand by and support your family. They are the only family you will ever have.
7. A soft answer turns away wrath. (Angry people can have the anger sapped out of them if you stay calm.)
8. Even though you may want to sleep in, when Mom says get up, get going!
9. Sneaking or hiding things from your mom and dad is never good.
10. No matter what you do, no matter how stupid your choices are, your mother and father will always love you.
11. And God loves you more than mom and Dad.
12. Don't do tomorrow what you can do today.

13. NEVER go to sleep mad, talk to someone.

I thought about how sometimes in life I didn't do the wise thing and chose to do something I knew was wrong. Sometimes that was as simple as putting off something I should be doing until tomorrow. You know that homework you were supposed to do, that you put off? You purposefully chose to hide or ignore? Well when you get older, how you deal with doing homework effects your work life. Getting things done on time can mean the difference between being a success and being what we call "a dollar short." Which would you rather have, a dollar in your pocket or owing someone that dollar in your pocket? Because when you have a job and do not do something on time, then you risk losing your job and getting fired.

Dear God,

Help me to obey my parents. Help me to know how important what they are teaching me is. Help me to be respectful and not rebellious, even when I think I am right. Help me to see why my parents say no when I want them to say yes.

Lord Jesus, help me to think on what my parents say to me about right and wrong. Help me to store those things in my heart, that I may be obedient to You also.

In Jesus Name, Amen.

DAY 39
PROVERBS 6:30-31

30 [Men] do not despise a thief, if he steals to satisfy his soul when he is hungry;

31 But [if] he be found, he shall restore sevenfold; he shall give all the substance of his house.

At some point in your life, you will encounter a thief. There are two kinds of thieves. 1) Those who must steal in order to live. 2) Those who steal for pleasure and because they believe you owe them.

As a young teen, an older teen tried to rob of me of my bike. He believed because I was skinny and did not look strong enough to beat him up it was his right to take my bike.

Well, imagine me believing that could be right. HAHA! Never happened. Would you believe someone had more of a right to what is yours than you who buy those things? Yes, it sounds ridiculous!

This would be robber pulled a knife to get my bike. I was smart enough to understand that it was important to put my bike between us. But to hold onto it. I also knew nothing is worth my life. If they have a weapon it pays to be able to live another day by giving what is yours to them.

This day God was generous to me. Two adults started to walk past us not paying attention to what was happening to me, or simply clueless to what was happening. This angered me. I said to them "When you get robbed don't expect me to help when I am walking by." The two people stopped. I don't know what I expected them to do. I don't know why I had to say this, but I did. The robber's head snapped at me he came closer with the knife and angrily yelled, "I can't believe you did that!" Then he ran away.

This was long before the idea of cell phones existed in most people's minds. I had to go to a stranger's house and ask to use their phone to call the police. The police took my description. They said, they knew who it was. They would be visiting his house.

I have met the other type of robber. A woman came to me as a manager of a McDonald's. She begged for food for her children. She was so scared of not having anything to feed them she was in tears as she came to me. She was scared her next choice was to go against God and rob someone so she could provide for her children. I listened to her story. I walked to where her children were in the Mickey Ds. She had four small children whose tummies were rumbling. They were doing their best to be good for their mom.

As a believer I knew it was right to feed her and her family. I also knew doing so could be seen as robbing my boss. So I counted out what I was giving them and wrote a note to my boss, offering to pay for the food if he needed me to do that. Then, I gave the mother and her children food. I gave them enough to be filled. The mother could not understand it, she expected to have to rob us or someone else to get what she needed. She told me this. I told her thank Jesus not me. She wanted to repay us for the food. I told her not to do this. But, at some time in the future, she should do the same to another person in need.

My boss told me I did not need to pay for the food. It was the only right thing to do. He also told me the woman came back thanking him.

Sadly, most of those I met in my life who are robbers, believe that the person they are robbing has too much stuff, so it is ok for them to take it. One robber I met after he came to Jesus. He said people would come after he robbed the place and would find nothing in their home. No couch, no furniture, nothing at all in the home. He felt no guilt. After all they had so much stuff.

In Proverbs it says that a robber owes 7 times the amount he stole when he is caught. We do not have a law that punishes like this. Do you think it would make people think if they knew this was a penalty?

Dear God,

Help me to love and praise you each day. For it is you who provides for me. You gave my parents talents so they can provide for me. You provided my parents with jobs. You taught my mother and father kindness and they share their love of You with me.

Lord, please help me to be generous to those in need. Please help me to see the difference in those who rob. Teach me to be wise so I may be able to give answers that You would like to see.

In Jesus Name, Amen.

DAY 40
PROVERBS 7:1-2

1 My son, keep my words, And treasure my commands within you.

2 Keep my commands and live, And my law as the apple of your eye.

The father once again is telling the son to keep his words. To really hold on to what he is saying to him.

Why? If the son keeps these wise words, he shall live. Life is a bit easier using wisdom. When you remember and use what you've been taught. How do I know? I'm living proof! One thing my father told me I never forgot. He said, "Do a good job and you'll always get respect". He was right! The result of what he said was not just respect...also, a job well done provides the good feeling that comes with that. It also makes your Father in heaven smile at you as well. The law being the apple of your eye means it's precious. It is very important and dear to you. It is very, very special. Please keep the Word to yourselves as valuable. Because it is!

Father,

Please help me to keep your Word special. Because I know it is very important. Your Word is wisdom. Your Word is full of life! Help me to hold it close. In my heart, my mind; and my spirit. Help me to live by what I hear.

In Jesus name I pray and thank You. Amen.

DAY 41
PROVERBS 7:3-4

3 Bind them on your fingers; Write them on the tablet of your heart,

4 Say to wisdom, "You are my sister", And call understanding your nearest kin.

Have you ever tied a string around your finger to remember something? This is a very old idea. Yet most people believed it worked. This is what they did in Bible times. They would tie portions of Scripture to themselves to remember it. The more you remember, the more you will know. Hopefully the more you know, the better you will live. Calling wisdom your sister is special. It shows how close you two are to each other. Sometimes we don't like to listen to our sisters. Yet you should always listen to wisdom. Understanding is not far from wisdom either. Wisdom and understanding walk hand in hand. You seldom have one without the other. They are related to each other. Soon they will be related to you. As you live through the two of them.

Father,

Help me to keep wisdom as close as a sister. Please help me to listen more to wisdom, and live by it. Please also help me to understand more of Your things and other things I don't yet know of.

In Jesus name I pray and thank You. Amen.

DAY 42
PROVERBS 8:1-11

1 Does not wisdom cry? and understanding put forth her voice?
2 She stands in the top of high places, by the way in the places of the paths.

3 She cries at the gates, at the entry of the city, at the coming in at the doors.

4 Unto you, O men, I call; and my voice [is] to the sons of man.

5 O you simple, understand wisdom: and, you fools, be you of an understanding heart.

6 Hear; for I will speak of excellent things; and the opening of my lips [shall be] right things.

7 For my mouth shall speak truth; and wickedness [is] an abomination to my lips.

8 All the words of my mouth [are] in righteousness; [there is] nothing difficult or perverse is in them.

9 They [are] all plain to him that understands, and right to them that find knowledge.

10 Receive my instruction, and not silver; and knowledge rather than choice gold.

11 For wisdom [is] better than rubies; and all the things that may be desired are not to be compared to it.

Do you ever think after you did something stupid, "Why did I do that? I knew better!" Doesn't that sound like wisdom crying in your ear? Now be honest, before you did the stupid thing, did you hear a small voice saying, "DON"T DO THAT!"

Sometimes wisdom cries. Crying here means saying something loud enough so everyone can hear. Towns used to

73

have a job called the "Town Crier." A man with this job would walk around town and make public announcements. This is before microphones and speakers. So, his voice had to be deep and booming.

This is why Wisdom stands in the high places. She stands where paths cross, she stands at the city gates, and the city walls. She offers her words to us freely and openly. We don't have to seek something hidden. This may seem a little strange, but there are those out there who want us to think some wisdom is hidden, that only they have this special wisdom. Wisdom is understanding. It gives you a special way to grasp the why and how, and sometimes even more.

It (wisdom) can help you see something coming down the road before it can even be seen. It's a pretty cool thing to be able to say a+b=c. You see *a* and you see *b*, not yet next to *a*, so you know *c* is coming. It's like seeing three boys you know who never seem to be apart, let's call them: Tom, Dick, and, Harry. You see Tom and look around guessing that Dick and Harry can't be far behind. You see Dick, but Harry cannot be seen. But you guess Harry will soon be there.

Not so impossible is it? Not very hidden also. That's the glory and beauty in wisdom. You start to put things together differently. You start to see what could be, not just what is.

Dear Jesus,

Thank you for sharing wisdom with us. Thank you for making wisdom something that is not hidden. Thank you for making wisdom something that announces itself. So, I must listen.

Lord, help me to listen and seek wisdom. Help me to begin to connect the dots, to see how things fit together. Lord grant me wisdom. It is what you want for me. I want this. Help me to seek you and learn from you.

In Jesus Name, Amen.

DAY 43
PROVERBS 8:12-16

12 I, wisdom dwell with caution, and find out knowledge of witty inventions.

13 The fear of the LORD [is] to hate evil: pride, and arrogancy, and the evil way, and the froward mouth, do I hate.

14 Counsel [is] mine, and sound wisdom: I [am] understanding; I have strength.

Wisdom is talking here. She tells us who she is. She starts with telling us who she lives with. Wisdom and caution dwell together. This is kind of like the saying, "think before you speak." If you think over what you say you will use wisdom, and caution will say, "I shouldn't say that, it will get me into trouble."

What is cool, is that some people use knowledge and wisdom to solve problems. They are called inventors. Today you have used a cell phone because someone used knowledge and wisdom to solve a problem. It's not that long ago they were a fantasy many thought impossible.

Vs. 13: It makes sense that if you fear God—if you love God, you will hate evil which is the opposite of God, and what desires you to be separated from God.

Pride can be good and bad. Good pride is when you are fussy so you can make something and make it well. My mother made the best apple pie. Mmm! It was something she would smile about. Pride as a bad thing, is being proud and unable to see how that proudness hurts you. Pride can stop your ears so you can't hear what others think, because your way is the best way, and no one can top that.

Vs. 14: When you want advice, you don't go to just anyone to get it. You pick the smart guy, the guy you think usually has the answer. You look for someone you place trust in to give you that answer. This is called seeking "counsel." Lawyers are called counselors. There are other professions you seek out for counseling also. You don't just go to anyone. You look to see if they are recommended. After all you don't want bad advice. You want someone whose understanding is STRONG and proven.

Lord Jesus,

Help me to recognize those around me who not only seek knowledge but seek your wisdom. I want to be wise. I want to grow in knowledge and learn how to use that knowledge in ways that would make my parents proud and you proud, God!

Help me God, for some things seem hard to me. Help me to fight to get that knowledge and wisdom. Help me to understand that the wisdom others attain may not be easy and in many ways be a struggle for me, BUT there is goodness in the fight within myself for knowledge and wisdom.

In Jesus Name, Amen.

DAY 44
PROVERBS 8:15-16

15 By me kings reign, and princes decree justice.

16 By me princes rule, and nobles, [even] all the judges of the earth.

To rule and do it right you must have some wisdom. Today, rulers are also called President or Prime Minister. Foolish leaders have to trust their advisors to make decisions. But what if the advisor is bad? What if he chooses to do bad things more than good things?

It is interesting that the passage mentions princes, nobles, and judges. The reason is simple. God is telling us that everyone over us in government must seek wisdom or be a failure.

This is another reason to pray for those over us in government. No one wants to be ruled be fools who put their foolishness on parade. Do fools get into public office? Yes. There is one who tried to make a law to stop cows from farting in the USA. Foolishness on parade is like watching an emperor walk down the street proudly proclaiming his clothes can only be seen by the wise, when in truth he is not wearing any clothes.

Dear God Almighty,

Help those over me to seek your wisdom even as I do. I want to be wise in you! I want my leaders, my future bosses, to be wise in Your word. Lord, even now help them to see their wisdom in calling on your name! Help me also never to forget that there is power and wisdom in your name.

In Jesus Name, Amen.

DAY 45
PROVERBS 8:17-21

17 I love them that love me; and those that seek me early shall find me.

18 Riches and honor [are] with me; [yea], durable riches and righteousness.

19 My fruit [is] better than gold, yea, than fine gold; and my revenue than choice silver.

20 I lead in the way of righteousness, in the midst of the paths of judgment:

21 That I may cause those that love me to inherit substance; and I will fill their treasures.

Verse 17 is about you! Wisdom loves them that love her. You are still young, it is still early in your life, and you are seeking her (wisdom)! So, you shall find her!

Verse 18--One of the things about wisdom is that when you get her, NO ONE and NO THING can take her from you. Wisdom is both granted and earned.

Some wisdom comes with age. It is why in some cultures the oldest people are held up as close to God. They call these people village elders. They go to them with questions and those elders answer with wisdom from having lived through many years. Sometimes the older people see patterns where the young cannot because they were not alive to see something that may look like it is repeating. As you grow older you will be able to see somethings like this. It will help you to see things that could happen before they do.

Verses 19-21--Wisdom also can give you rewards. Some of these rewards can save you from getting into trouble. Wisdom can save your life by sometimes having you say "no" or "yes" to something. This is because our answers, our choices, can affect the rest of our lives. This may seem hard to believe now. As you grow older you will grasp just how big a small choice can be in your life.

A friend recently reminded me of an old saying, "you can take that to the bank." This was usually said about someone's honesty, or their person (character) being of such goodness that it had value. She was saddened that you don't really hear this anymore. The truth was that someone who was honest, and whom you believed in (had good character), could get a loan easily. It was something that had great financial value! After all, you wouldn't loan someone $100 if you do not believe in them or their ability to earn more and pay it back.

Revenue is income---usually we think of that as money in your wallet or the bank! Revenue can also be what you store in yourself, such as wisdom and knowledge. That is the stuff far more valuable than silver and gold.

But just to be clear here, verse 21 is talking about the kind of reward you can put in your wallet or bank. This is a promise from God to you, if you seek His wisdom and glory that you will not be someone who lives in want or lack.

What a glorious generous God we serve. He asks us to choose to follow Him. He gives us wisdom when we seek her. Those two choices, can "put money in the bank." Isn't this more reason to work to gain wisdom? YES IT IS!

Dear God,

Thank you for loving me so much! Your death on the cross for MY sins is so huge. It is something I can never repay. Yet, you go beyond this, because you are so generous. You bless us with wisdom. I am young and seeking wisdom. I am seeking her early and thank you knowing you made a promise to give me wisdom because I am young and seeking her!

Lord, help me to see the wisdom and ask my elders questions when I do not know the answers. Help me to not be a "Know-It-All." Help me to seek wisdom from those around me whose character I can "take to the bank." Help me to thank my mother and father for being people whom I trust and giving me the example of whom I should I be. Bless them for this.

In Jesus Name—Amen.

DAY 46
PROVERBS 8:22-31

22 The LORD possessed me in the beginning of his way, before his works of old.

23 I was set up from everlasting, from the beginning, or ever the earth was.

24 When [there were] no depths, I was brought forth; when [there were] no fountains abounding with water.

25 Before the mountains were settled, before the hills was I brought forth:

26 While as yet he had not made the earth, nor the fields, nor the highest part of the dust of the world.

27 When he prepared the heavens, I [was] there: when he set a compass upon the face of the depth:

28 When he established the clouds above: when he strengthened the fountains of the deep:

29 When he gave to the sea his decree, that the waters should not pass his commandment: when he appointed the foundations of the earth:

30 Then I was by him, [as] one brought up [with him]: and I was daily [his] delight, rejoicing always before him;

31 Rejoicing in the habitable part of his earth; and my delights [were] with the sons of men.

Were you surprised to find out that wisdom is older than the creation of man? That she is older than the creation of heavens? That wisdom was there when God set clouds in the sky? I know it made me think.

Amazing stuff! We are often told to respect our elders. So, does this mean we should respect wisdom because she is our elder? Yes! Even more important, she was created and was present during the creation of the earth. She was with God. This tells us that there is something so deep and important about wisdom in that it comes from God alone. Only God creates wisdom. Only God allows us to become wise. This is why God is the grantor of wisdom to them that diligently seek her.

It is another reason why those who are wise should be respected. Think of a wise person, as someone who somehow obtained favor in God's eyes and that He shared something with them that was created before mankind. This truly means that a wise person deserves respect.

***

Dear God,

Help me to seek your wisdom, help me to honor her and to recognize that it is You, and You alone, who created wisdom and grant her to those that seek her.

Lord, help me to show respect to my elders and give the ability to seek wisdom and understanding from my elders. Help me to listen and learn tidbits of knowledge from them that I may store it away to be used later.

Thank you, Lord for loving me so! In Jesus Name, Amen.

DAY 47
PROVERBS 8:33-36

33 Hear instruction, and be wise, and refuse it not.

34 Blessed [is] the man that hears me, watching daily at my gates, waiting at the posts of my doors.

35 For whosoever finds me finds life, and shall obtain favor of the LORD.

36 But he that sins against me wrongs his own soul: all they that hate me love death.

***

One of the most important things to recognize if you want to be wise, is that God gave us two ears and one mouth. We should be listening more often than we talk. If we listen more than we have to respond with our mouths, we will not be refusing wisdom.

One of my life lessons, was that "I do not have to respond to someone every time with words." This loving God of ours gave us ways to show each other that we are listening, and that we care about what is being said. Non-verbal communication is just as important as when we open our mouths and say, "Yes that is interesting." What do we not say to communicate our interest in what someone is saying?

- Lean forward
- Sit on the edge of the seat
- Maintain eye contact or watch very closely

Ask yourself what else do you do to show interest in what your parents or a teacher is telling you? How do you show you are interested? Do you ask questions later to check to make sure you understood something? Do you come prepared to listen? In school that means did you come with a pen or pencil? Did you start the day with a good breakfast so you can listen?

It is something special to find a person, you want to learn from. It is like finding a precious gem you can never touch but want so much to hold in your hands. At that moment, you realize you must do what you can to make that possible.

You also do not want to make that person disappointed. You will do things they ask. You want them to see you as better than you sometimes see yourself.

Wisdom calls out to listen. If we love our lives then we must listen. Strangely, there are those who do not love their lives. They love death. The Bible says that "there is no greater love than that seen when a man lays down his life for another." That love can be shown for his life and the life of another in that he gives his life to protect another. But a man who loves death---he does not protect when he gives up his life.

Lord Jesus,

Help me to be an active listener. Help me to listen more. Help me to be someone who shows I have interest in what my parents and teachers say. I need to listen to become wise. That is what You want for me, so help me to do this God.

Jesus, I know you love me! I know you do because you gave up your life to protect my eternal life. You died so I could be free from the penalty of sin. Help me to live as someone who loves life. Help me to live as an example of your love. Help me to be the one who You choose to show others how great You are by the way I live my life.

In Jesus name, Amen.

DAY 48
PROVERBS 9:1-6

1 Wisdom has built her house, She has hewn out her seven pillars:
2 She has slaughtered her meat, She has mixed her wine, She has also furnished her table.
3 She has sent out her maidens, She cries out from the highest places of the city,
4 "Whoever is simple, let him turn in here!" As for him who lacks understanding, she says to him,
5 "Come, eat of my bread and drink of the wine I have mixed.
6 Forsake foolishness and live, And go in the way of understanding."

———————————————————————

Wisdom here is preparing for something. She is making ready a feast. A great feast or dinner for some special guests, those who have a need of what she has. It is not the food mainly that she gives, it is the advice she desires to share. Why? To turn people from going the wrong way. To give them the understanding they need for life. Also, to keep them from trouble. She cries out from the top of the city. So that she can be heard by everyone. What she has to share is very important. At the end of the passage today, she gives a command to leave foolishness alone. She commands you to put foolishness far away, so that you may have an easier time at life. Life has problems of its own. Keeping foolishness close will only add to them.

———————◇———————

Father,

Please help me to pay attention to wisdom. Help me to hear her speak to me. Help me to understand what she tells me. Please give me the strength and courage to do it.

I pray and thank You in Jesus name. Amen.

DAY 49
PROVERBS 9:7

7 He who corrects a scoffer gets shame for himself, And he rebukes a wicked man only harms himself.

———————◇———————

Ever tried to tell someone they're wrong when they don't want to hear it? It's hard. Doing this can cause the other person to begin insulting you. They may even attempt to make you look bad in front of others. This is really embarrassing. So, be careful on who and how you correct someone. It may come back to you in a negative way, and we don't want that.

———————◇———————

Father,

Please help me to know when to speak when I see something wrong. Give me the courage to do so when I have to. Help me to say nothing when it is not needed.

I pray and thank You, in Jesus name. Amen.

DAY 50
PROVERBS 9:8

8 Do not correct a scoffer, lest he hates you; Rebuke a wise man and he will love you.

When you correct someone who doesn't care, they will not like you nor appreciate your attempt to set them right. They might even hate you as the Bible says.

So, please know when to speak and when to keep silent. If you don't it can be hurtful and embarrassing. If you tell someone who is wise when they are wrong, they will appreciate it. They may even thank you. They will love you for it. Why? Because they know that your correction is a sign of caring about them. It says that you want the best for them.

Father,

Please keep me from scoffers. Those who don't care about how I feel or what I think or say. Help me to have wisdom on when I should correct someone. Lord, please direct me to those who are willing to hear it and learn.

I pray and thank You in Jesus name. Amen.

DAY 51
PROVERBS 9:9

9 Give [instruction] to a wise [man], and he will be still wiser; Teach a just [man], and he will increase in learning.

Instruction comes in a variety of ways. Sometimes it comes like directions on how to put something together. Sometimes, instruction comes with someone guiding you to do something correctly. Sometimes instruction comes with correction. Sometimes, "No, that is wrong," can be used to help you learn what is right. A wise person will absorb (take in) instruction. He knows it will help him, so he listens and uses the instruction to become a better person.

You have had students in your class who seem to act like vacuum cleaners whenever something new is taught. He/She wants to learn everything. They seem to quickly learn everything while some of us have to work to learn everything. Then there is the kid who loves being the class clown, and the kid who likes being annoying. Neither want to improve themselves. They just want attention. Which are you?

Lord Jesus,

Help me to be like the wise man, seeking instruction and learning to make myself better. Help me to see the good in learning new things. Help me to see how I can use things in the future.

Lord help me not to distract others from learning. Learning is something you admire in us.

In Jesus name, Amen.

DAY 52
PROVERBS 9:10

10 The fear of the Lord is the beginning of wisdom,
And the knowledge of the Holy One is understanding.

To fear someone or something is to give it respect. In nature, lightning should be feared and respected. Why? Because, it's powerful, dangerous; and deadly. Water is also to be respected. When there's a lot of it, it can be powerful, too! Fearing God is the beginning of wisdom. He is always the most important person you respect first! He is more powerful than lightning, water or any other thing we know of! It's the beginning of wisdom because it's the smartest thing to do. Also, as we grow in knowing God, we can begin to understand Him more...just like finding things out you never knew of your family or friends. The more you find out and know about Him, the more you will understand Him.

Father,

Please teach me to fear You and to respect You more and more. Help me to always do what You say. Please help me to know You more. So that I may understand Your ways.

I pray and thank You in Jesus name. Amen.

DAY 53
PROVERBS 9:11

11 For by me your days will be multiplied, and years of life will be added to you.

You can live longer by knowing God. Those who lived in early Bible times did. How? They knew who to respect and obey. They knew exactly who to listen to. I would like to live as long as I can. How about you?

If it's the Lord's will, I want to be playing my bass guitar for a very long time! Because I love music! How about you? What would you like to live long enough to see? The Bible tells you another way to add years to your life. Do you know what that is? It's one of the Ten Commandments. "Honor your father and your mother, that your days may be long upon the land which the Lord your God is giving you." (Exodus 20:12).

Father,

Please add years to my life that I may see good things and also to do a lot for You. Help me to honor and respect my parents more. Help me to hear, understand and do what they say so that what I'm asking you will happen.

I pray and thank You in Jesus name. Amen.

DAY 54
PROVERBS 9:12

12 If you are wise. you are wise for yourself, and if you scoff, you will bear it alone.

If you are wise, it is to your own benefit. It will help you through the hard times you will face in life. This can also keep you out of trouble, if you use it correctly. On the other hand, if you scoff or make fun of something, it can be embarrassing - especially at times when you may not know what you are talking about. That embarrassment will only be on yourself, and no one wants to look foolish. Do they? So be careful not to mock or make fun of anyone or anything. It might come back on you.

Father,

Please help me to be wise. Help me to use that wisdom well, so that I can stay out of trouble. Lord, please help me that I may not make You or my parents angry.

I pray and thank You in Jesus name. Amen.

DAY 55
PROVERBS 10:1

1 The proverbs of Solomon. A wise son makes a glad father: but a foolish son [is] the heaviness of his mother.

Some of these things are truly hard to grasp until you become a parent. You can get how a wise son makes his father glad, but do you understand how a fool weighs heavy on his mother?

Mom's do a lot of worrying about you. It is part of how God made them. It is part of how they love you. Have you ever thought about how when you do something foolish your mother stores it in her heart? She does not do this to remember and laugh later. She does this because it is the way God made her. She thinks on all the things you do...not just the foolish things. Her heart rejoices when you succeed and pass a test. Her heart jumps up and down with you when you do something right for the first time. So, when you do something foolish, it is not like an ornament you hang on a Christmas tree. It is like a weight that pulls and tugs on her happiness. As you grow up, Moms expect you to do foolish things. It is part of growing up. After all, us boys do the stupid things. But when you, more often than not, do the foolish things, then those little weights from memories become a burden to your mother.

Mothers tend to like things like necklaces. If her memories of you are pieces of a necklace then your good and wise deeds will be like fine jewels, while your foolish deeds will be like ugly fishing weights. Fishing weights can be made of lead. Lead is not something pretty - it's purpose is usually heaviness, not prettiness. If your mom's necklace is made of lead for all your foolish things, you are making heavy memories for your mother.

Think before you act. For some of us being impulsive---doing what we think, comes naturally. Sometimes it comes so quickly we really didn't think---we just did it! Oh no! That's when Moms and Dads say, "You need to think before you act," and you need to think before you open your mouth."

Dear God,

Help me to do the wise things. Help me to be a person who thinks before he acts. Help me to show my love for my parents by choosing to do the right things, the good things, and the wise things. Lord Jesus, please help me to make those good and wise choices.

Lord, thank you for parents who love and guide me in what is wise, good, and right. Thank you for relatives who encourage me to seek you. Thank you for friends who love you and want me to do what is wise, and good, and right.

In Jesus Name, Amen.

DAY 56
PROVERBS 10:2

2 Treasures of wickedness profit nothing: but righteousness delivers from death.

One of the largest robberies in US History happened in Rochester, NY. People took something like $7 million dollars from Brinks Armoured Car Service and were on the run. Things seemed to go well for them. No one seemed to know who did it. Police had an idea about one of them but had no proof. Almost a year later they were all still free. They had millions and could not spend one dollar because the serial numbers on the money had been recorded. They could probably swim in it but nothing more. One year after the robbery, three of them were arrested and a good amount of the cash was discovered. So, their ill-gotten gain earned them nothing but jail time.

Sometimes serving God means making the tough choices of doing right even when doing wrong is so much easier. Choosing to eat a healthy meal would be the right choice instead of making a meal from a small bag of cheese puffs, soda, some Doritos, and a Hershey Bar. What you eat is called your diet. Eating the healthy foods instead of the sugary and tempting treats can help you live longer. Diabetes, high blood pressure, and so many more bad things can shorten life. Choosing the right thing can make you live longer.

Dear God,

Help me to choose the good things and not the easy things. Help me to store up treasures in heaven that would make you proud of me.

Lord Jesus, guide me in your righteousness. Help me to see what is true and good.

In Jesus Name, Amen.

DAY 57
PROVERBS 10:3

3 The LORD will not allow the soul of the righteous to famish: but he casts away the substance of the wicked.

One of the most wonderful things about reading the Bible is the nuggets of wisdom that are told to us again and again in different ways. This passage talks about your life after death. There is a reward and a punishment waiting, based on a singular decision. Did you choose to make Jesus lord of your life?

Without Jesus all of what we do and say adds up to nothing, when we are talking about getting into heaven. With Jesus, all of what we do and say is to His benefit AND OURS. When we do what is right in His eyes, we are storing away precious gems in heaven. We are making "treasure" in heaven. That can be as simple as taking the garbage out like mom asked the first time and not the fourth time, doing your homework and turning it on time, or telling a friend about the loving God you serve.

Dear God,

Help me to store up treasures in heaven. I have a whole life ahead to make treasures for You! Help me to make the right and good choices that I may store up treasures in heaven.

Lord, help me to do what I am asked, help me to do what I should when I should.

In Jesus Name, Amen.

DAY 58
PROVERBS 10:4

4 Lazy hands make for poverty, but diligent hands bring wealth.

A lazy person sees a difficult task and steps back and looks at it asking how can I get out of this?

A diligent person sees a difficult task and steps back looking closely at the task. He takes out tools and measures what must be done from every angle. Then he starts the task with an intensity because he can see the end!

One day a teacher started a reading contest, a challenge to see who would read the most books. Everyone was excited. Oh, they had some clues as to who would win. They looked at each of their classmates guessing. Then they knew who would not win also, the lazy ones.

The contest began! Every student had to fill out a report for each book they read and then share it with the teacher and often with the class. Several students soon left the rest of the class behind. They had read 20 or more books while the others were struggling to reach 10.

Then the top three emerged – they had read 48 books and written reports. The class began to get excited wondering who would win in the end.

The person who did win ended up reading 10 more books than anyone else. The prize the teacher had offered was exciting. But she promised a secret reward that only the winner would know. The students waited on the edge of their seats to learn what that prize was.

The day came when the teacher handed the prize to the winner. She said the secret reward comes from the DILIGENCE of the winner. He did not put off reading once. He kept at it every day. His secret reward is KNOWLEDGE that no one can ever take from him. The teacher turned and looked at all of her students. She asked the winner, if he found this an easy win.

He answered, "Oh no, Miss. I wanted to go play games – but instead I read. I would take books with me in the car to read. Books went with us on vacation. It seems the more I read, the more I wanted to know.

Dear Lord,

Help me to be a hard worker. Help me to be diligent. Teach me how to do this. I want to find my place in the world, a place where I can soar! Help me to be the hard worker, the one who honors you with my work.

Lord Jesus, help me not to put off things I should do. Help me not to be lazy. Help me instead choose to be one who works hard.

In Jesus Name, Amen.

DAY 59
PROVERBS 10:5

5 He that gathers in summer [is] a wise son: [but] he that sleeps in harvest [is] a son that causes shame.

One thing I have learned over the years is that God repeats what he thinks is important. When people give sermons, they repeat the most important thing 3 times. When your parents want to communicate something important, they say it so many times, that when you are old, you can't help but repeat it to your own children. Proverbs warns of the dangers of laziness a lot. Maybe it is because it is part of being human to want to take it easy. Maybe it's because God knows how good it feels to relax and enjoy your day off.

Laziness is not getting up by setting your own alarm and waiting until mom or dad wake you. Yes, I am saying if you're reading this book, it's time to start setting your own alarm clock to wake up. Laziness is not offering to help when you see someone doing something YOU KNOW they could use help in. Some people are too stubborn to ask for help. We have to rise up and be bigger. We have to offer to help even when someone is not asking. This is a lesson I learned later and am passing on to you. Just catching this lesson, will have your father think of you better.

This book was written thinking of boys who mostly are not living on farms. A boy on a farm who does not help in the harvest makes it harder for the father to ask the community for help when he needs it. The father would be ashamed to admit his own boy wouldn't help him.

Shame is something we never want to cause our fathers to feel. We want them to be proud of us! We want our Dad's to look at us with pride and smile as they say to others, "THAT IS MY BOY!" "THAT IS MY SON!"

Dear Lord Jesus!

Please help me to be a person who sees when others need help. Help me then to be the one who offers to help. I want to be an example of YOU! You help me in so many ways. Please let me be that type of person to others.

Lord God, help me to make my parents proud. Help me to be the one they know they can depend on. Help me to be helpful.

In Jesus name, Amen.

DAY 60
PROVERBS 10:6

6 Blessings [are] upon the head of the just: but violence covers the mouth of the wicked.

Some wisdom comes with age. Understanding this passage is one of those things. As an older person who taught in schools many years, I can say that I have seen many students who do what is right because they choose to follow what is right and just. They may not all serve God, but on these students, there are great blessings towards a successful future.

The part about "violence covering the mouth of the wicked," would have left me confused at your age, after all, how can violence cover a mouth?

The answer is found in Matthew 12:34 and Luke 6:35, when Jesus was talking to a bunch of selfish self-serving leaders of the Jews. He said, "O generation of vipers, how can you, being evil, speak good things? for out of the abundance of the heart the mouth speaks."

When a person's heart has nothing but badness, violence readily is expressed by that person's mouth. You could say violence sits on the tongue of such a person. As a teacher I saw this in students who so easily issued physical threats from their mouths before even knowing they had done this. These students grew up angry at the world. They hated everyone. They were ready to strike out at anyone and anything should a chance come.

Now, let's go back to the first part of the verse -- the blessing. What did Jesus say to those whose words and actions were the opposite of violence? "Blessed are the peace makers, for they shall be called the children of God" (Matthew 5:9). True peace brings calm to your soul. It comes from knowing Jesus. To bring peace to others is to share Jesus!

Dear Jesus,

I have friends who need you! I know of others I would not call friend who need the love you offer. They need that loving calmness you give my soul. Take them from wickedness. Help them to leave it and find you!

Lord God, please help me to be the bait that draws them to you. Help me to live as your example. Help me to be the one that shines like a beacon to them. Guard my words and actions, so others may see the blessings in following You!

In Jesus Name, Amen.

DAY 61
PROVERBS 10:7

7 The memory of the righteous [is] blessed, But the name of the wicked will rot.

Humans love examples. We love to see people who do things right so we can understand better. Some people became legends where some of the stories about a person are not always true, but they have that tidbit of truth that are told to tell you about the character of a person. Do you remember the story of George Washington and the cherry tree? Supposedly the first Constitutional president of the USA chopped down a cherry tree and his father got mad seeing the cherry tree cut down, and asked **"who cut this tree down?"** "George is said to have answered, "Father, I cannot tell a lie. It was me who did it." Supposedly, this is not a true story about George Washington. But it is a tale about the man's character. It tells generations of American's that President Washington was an honest man. There are stories about the honesty of Abraham Lincoln also. The stories about his honesty are actually true.

Do you want to be set up as an example of righteousness? Do you want to be the one who sets the standard by which many are shown right from wrong? Or, do you want to be the one who is forgotten? We forget the names of those who do not measure up. We don't talk about those who were wealthy and evil. We talk about people who were examples of goodness, and those whose who stood up as examples of what to doright.

From George Washington's time, one name stands out as an example of "evil," that is Benedict Arnold. Benedict Arnold was a man who's named is remembered for turning against his country. His name was so cursed from his evil actions, only those who are ignorant of history would name their children after him.

Which do you want to be? A person who's name brings smiles and good thoughts, or a person whose name can be easily forgotten or worse, a man whose name is remembered for his evil.

Dear Lord,

Help me to become a man whose name when said, makes people think of you. Help me to grow into being a man my mother and father are proud to say, "that is my son."

Lord God, you know my heart. You know when I desire to do wrong and when I desire to do right. You even hear my thoughts. Help me to seek your will for my life. Help me to choose Your way and not my own, that my name be become blessed.

In Jesus Name, Amen.

DAY 62
PROVERBS 10:8

8 The wise in heart will receive commands, But a chattering fool will fall.

A command is not something you should do. It is something you must do. A command is something you have no choice in; it is something you have no voice in. Yet, your heart should easily recognize when a command is good. The wise heart sees commands that are good as beneficial. Sometimes you may look at a command as a large amount of work. It may even look to be over your ability. Overwhelming!

When teachers hand out homework, it is a command. Not a suggestion. There are penalties when you do not do the work assigned. A wise heart knows the importance in doing homework and receives that assignment.

Parents and teachers alike have a favorite saying. It is something ingrained into us. "God gave you two ears and one mouth for a reason. You should listen twice as much as you talk." If you're talking, can you hear the command? Even if you do, will you remember it if you are talking a lot? Truth is, this becomes difficult.

Sometimes it is the need of a person to respond to everything that is said that makes a person seem a fool. This is not an easy thing to avoid. Wisdom tells us to listen more than we talk. Wisdom tells us to receive commands. It does not tell us to open our mouths and respond to every little thing. Even when we want to. Sometimes it is best to hold our tongue...especially when we get mad.

Lord Jesus,

Help me to be listen to the commands given to me. Help me to see your goodness in them. Help me to see receiving these commands as your wisdom for me.

Lord God, help me not to respond to every little thing. Help me to listen more than I talk. Lord, help me to be a good a listener and doer of your Word.

In Jesus Name, Amen.

DAY 63
PROVERBS 10:9

9 He that walks uprightly walks surely: but he that perverts his ways shall be known.

Those who set the example of following Jesus in all they do earn a reputation of trust and honor. Think of those who you know who stand as examples to you and your parents. Who do you think of together? Ask your parents what makes them think those people are examples of following Jesus, who stand out?

The opposite here is a person who "perverts" his ways. "Perverting" something is making something straight, crooked. These are the people whom you know act in such a way that would make Jesus sad. They may deny Jesus exists. They may do drugs or drink so much alcohol, that they have difficulty understanding they have a serious problem.

This proverb mentions one thing behind it all. One thing that causes the good deeds versus the bad deeds. That one thing is a choice. People make choices every day on what to say and how to act. Your choices today, can affect how people see you tomorrow.

Look at it in terms of doing your homework. Will people trust that you will do your homework, if yesterday you did your homework, but today you do not?

———————————————————————

Lord Jesus,

Please help me to make good choices. Help me to make wise choices. I want to be the person who walks uprightly, I want my choices to set me apart as an example of serving you.

Great King Jesus, guide me that my words and deeds cause me to become the bait that draws many to you.

In Jesus name, Amen.

DAY 64
PROVERBS 10:10

10 He who winks with the eye causes trouble, but a prating fool will fall.

———————————————————————

The first part of this verse seems weird. Yes, I said weird. It doesn't seem something we should expect, and that tells us we need to know more. So, I looked up what they mean by winking. Sometimes translating is not enough, you need to understand culture and sayings. Winking here means "one who does not take wickedness seriously."

You are going to meet people like this as you grow older. A person who does not seem to fear or care about the dangers of wickedness is like the one who sees something tempting to try "just once."

Story below:

- --

There were three boys walking down the path which God had set for them. God had even put lights on the path so that they would not lose their way. The three boys laughed and played on the path, but never straying from it. Nothing seemed as beautiful as where they were. Nothing seemed as good as where they were. When each of them on their own found the path, they heard this beautiful music like angels singing. Each of them had no reason to leave the path God had set for them. Now they had each other. They had the joy of Christian friendship to assist them on their path.

As the boys walked onward, they noticed a man on the side of the path sleeping. He became excited seeing the boys. He ran to them and talked excitedly of the candy shop he had just been to. Every dreamy concept of sugar you could imagine was there. Chocolate, caramel, peppermint, spearmint, fruity flavors and so, so, much more.

As all three boys listened their tummies began to rumble as they each thought of their favorite candy.

Then the man pointed off the path to the candy shop. It was beautiful! Even the outside of the shop looked good enough to eat, with large pictures of yummy candies.

The oldest boy said, "We shouldn't leave the path."

The next oldest boy said, "But it looks so yummy and it's not so far off we can't see the lit path we are on.

The youngest boy was only thinking of his love of sweets. But he would do what the older boys decided.

The two older boys argued and argued. Then the boy arguing to try the candy shop stopped arguing and started to walk on the grass and off towards candy store.

The older boy went to grab him and warn him even more about the dangers of leaving this path. He missed----so he ran towards his friend who had left the path to catch him.

The boy who chose to try the candy shop started to run sticking his tongue out saying don't worry. It's not far off. I can find my way back. When the older boy and the youngest one met again on the path they stood and watched their friend step onto the porch of the store. ----Then SLAM A CAGE WALL APPEARED, TRAPPING HIM!

The boy who seems to laugh at wickedness brought trouble. The two other boys had to decide whether to leave the path to help their friend or to stay on it.

The "prating fool" in verse 10 is also the boy who races off God's path to check out the candy shop. He did what he wanted despite being warned. In the end he was trapped. He was the one who had fallen victim.

Dear Jesus,
Help me to keep my eyes on You and not stray from the path which you set before me. Keep me strong. Help me to grow in Your Word. Help me to choose to seek your will so I may not end up like the prating fool.

In Jesus Name, Amen.

DAY 65
PROVERBS 10:11

11 The mouth of a righteous [man is] a well of life: but violence covers the mouth of the wicked.

In all the things a righteous man does he uses his mouth to express ideas first. His ideas and his kind words bring life to those around him. Think of how the kind words of another whom you trust meant a lot to you. They made you smile so much it warmed you down to your heart.

The second part of this verse has violence covering the mouth. This part seems confusing, but it is actually pretty clear. There are people with evil in their hearts who hide what they want to do with kind and flattering words. They use nice words to cover up what they have done and what they intend to do. It is interesting that a person with an evil heart can express kind words at all. But the fact that the kind words are used to disguise and hide their evil should be a warning.

Think of a bully who says something like "I am going to take your toothache away." You know he intends to punch you in the face. His kind words are a mask for an evil deed.

Lord Jesus,

I beg of you make my words a reflection of your goodness. May they then bring life to others. Help me to use my words for good.

Sweet Jesus, please help me to choose my words wisely. I do not want to be wicked. I do not want to be the one who hides what I want to do with words that hide wickedness. Lord, I want my words to bring forth life. Shape my words Lord, guide them. That they may bring joy to others.

In Jesus Name, Amen.

DAY 66
PROVERBS 10:12

12 Hatred stirs up strife, But love covers all sins.

At some point in your life, you are going to meet people who seem happiest when others are fighting. These peoples sit back and watch. Today they even video it and put on YouTube. It takes a special kind of person to cause two people to come to blows. This person will go to one man and say. X over there said your mother is a --------. Then, while the first guy is stewing and saying out loud no one can say things about my mom and get away with it, he goes to X, that man who he claims insulted the other man's mother. He says, did you know Y said nasty things about your Mom and you are too wimpy to do anything about it. That person then sits back and watches and the two people who may have been friends before now come to blows.

In the church this type of person says things that get people to not trust each other.

What causes a person to do these things? Hatred. Holding that awful feeling in your heart blackens it, it makes your being feel dark and evil.

Now the person whose heart is full of the love that Jesus gives them does something different. He tells others about this man named Jesus and how he came to give his life that others may be forgiven of their sins.

Which person do you want to be? The person who holds love in his heart encourages others to have love and be loved, while the one whose heart is full of hatred stirs up others to have hatred in their hearts towards each other.

The person who teaches others to love is remembered with fondness and a smile. Ask your parents who taught them to love and watch their face light up with a smile and expect a story. Don't you want to be remembered this way? The other person is too easily forgotten.

Dear Lord God,

Help me to seek after your will. Help me to become a man whose love of you is known. Help me to be a boy who draws others to you by my words and deeds. I want to be remembered with a smile for sharing your love with others. Guide me to do that. Give me the right time and your words to do this.

In Jesus Name, Amen.

DAY 67
PROVERBS 10:13

13 In the lips of him that has understanding wisdom is found: but a rod [is] for the back of him that is void of understanding.

Yes, this passage explains why someone gets punished by being spanked or paddled. The purpose is to drive understanding into a child. A toddler with no understanding of the danger of a burner on a stove may try to put his hands on the pretty fire. Every time that child gets close a parent will say no and move the child away from the stove. Then after three or more tries at correction by redirecting, the child is spanked. Understanding suddenly appears! "If I touch this it can give me pain." The first thought may be that if I touch this I get spanked. But this is enough for the child to understand there is danger.

We boys do stupid things. Sometimes our stupidity earns us more than we want. We climb trees not thinking of dangers. We race around not caring about anything other than winning the race, even if we are losing it. Sometimes we just choose to do something we know we shouldn't. It is not like we do not know some of these things will make our parents not happy with our actions, and maybe disappointed in our choices too.

A spanking or paddling is to correct us. It is supposed to help us gain understanding. Some boys need more of this correction than others to get away from the void of understanding. A void is like a dark whole with no light. We need light.

We need to be examples of understanding, not examples of the dark void unable to be the bait that draws men to Jesus.

Think of this passage as a way God communicates his love to us. Correction shows us God wants us to be better. He wants us to be examples of wisdom not foolishness. Think of how you can be an example of wisdom not foolishness.

Lord Jesus,

I beg of you help me to truly seek to be a person of wisdom and not a person who needs correction. I know it is my parents' job to help me learn wisdom by correcting me and at times spanking me. Lord, thank you for parents who love me so much they want me to leave foolishness behind.

In Jesus Name, Amen.

DAY 68
PROVERBS 10:14

14 Wise [men] lay up knowledge: but the mouth of the foolish [is] near destruction.

As a writer, one of the things I do is a lot of research. The funny thing about doing research, is you learn how much you do not know. Every time I seek to learn more, I learn there is more I do not know. Think of it like a brick wall. Each time I learn there is something I do not know and seek to learn that something, I am adding another brick to the wall. The wall grows stronger and taller as I seek to know more. The funny thing is that as I seek to know more, I learn how much more I really do not know.

The second part of this verse reminds me of students who so quickly get themselves into trouble with their mouths. I had a student whose mom was a nice woman and never cursed. She prayed for her son every day. That student would leave to go to school and not get on the bus. Oh, he would come later after hanging with other kids who cuss and talk meanly. It became part of him to talk like his friends do. In school, he responded to me, his teacher, like he would his friends, with cussing and violence in his word choice. That choice of words led to his being suspended.

We often are the worst causes of our destruction. A fool will lay traps for himself, unknowingly. It's like a person who is concerned about bear traps, and puts out traps to protect himself, but puts the traps on his own path and not the one the bear takes. Soon the fool finds himself caught in his own trap.

Lord Jesus,

Help me to be a seeker of your Word. Help me to desire to know you and not be satisfied with what I know. Create a desire in me to know more! Knowing You is the foundation of wisdom, the layer upon which I can build.

God, please give me a great desire to learn more. So that I may serve you in new and greater ways.

In Jesus Name, Amen.

DAY 69
PROVERBS 10:15

15 The rich man's wealth [is] his strong city: the destruction of the poor [is] their poverty.

One thing you may never see in your life is a wealthy man complaining that he has too much money. Wealthy people create more than one stream of income. They invest in different things to bring them more money just in case something fails. This is like building a strong city with walls.

When the Bible was written a strong city had walls around it to protect the people within. The cities then were seen as strong if their walls that could stand up to those who attacked.

A man with much money would be protected. Safe.

You may never see a wealthy man complain of being a rich, but it is a guarantee that you will see a poor man complaining of being poor. The poor man complains. They see poverty as being their destruction. They see themselves as born into poverty and can never rise out of it.

In many countries, this is true today. However, in America and Canada any man can change his "station in life." A poor man can become wealthy! Will complaining change who you are? In America, would accepting being poor and believing you can never be more than poor be worse? How hard would that person work?

In America we teach children from the time they are born that they are the ones who determine their own station in life. What you put into making who you are, starting from what you put into doing your schoolwork and chores at home will affect how you live.

Do you complain about having homework and chores? Or, do you get them done quickly and then think about what more you can do because they are done? What would it mean to you, if you thought like this:

> If I mowed the lawn, and the neighbor's lawn was not mowed, maybe I could get permission from my parents to use the mower to earn extra cash. Then you earn $20 more!

Dear Jesus!

Help me to build up wealth by not being a complainer and instead becoming a doer. Help me to see a world of possible, a world where I can change things for the better.

Lord God, help me to see the importance in being part of the solution. Help me to see the ease in getting things done and the power and value in what I can do when they are done on time. I know my parents and teachers wish this for me. So Lord, please bless them for trying to teach this to me.

In Jesus name, Amen.

DAY 70
PROVERBS 10:16

16 The labor of the righteous [tends] to life: the fruit of the wicked to sin.

It is interesting as life passes by to watch others and where they find themselves later in life. Sometimes this is very sad.

Sometimes you get so excited meeting someone you know who will soar later on.

How can you tell? Well this Proverb is the real answer. The labor of the righteous. Who is righteous? Only Jesus. Our righteousness was purchased by his sacrifice for our sins. Knowing this don't we owe our lives to Him?

I once had a student whose approach to learning and politeness got teachers excited. I remember this student very well as I now see him in church every week. He had something called drive. He wanted to pass, he wanted to do better. Oh, he was not in love with school. He had his bad days also, but there was something in the way he talked to people and did his work, that told us all he was working towards something good. That man became a leader in the church! Funny thing, back then, he was not a Christian. God was working on Him and many of us could see it.

Then there is the work of the wicked. The truly sad thing here is the wicked don't see very far off in the future. They only see the "excitement" in their next sin. They will plan for it. They will work towards it. They do not see the dangers in living a life without Jesus. They only see the short-term pleasure in the sin they want to commit.

We owe it to Jesus to be better.

Dear Jesus!

Please, please make me into someone who sees the joy in serving you is far better than the pleasure in sin. Help me to see the joy in building towards a future with You! Help me to see the pleasure in meeting a goal that will make me into a better person for You!

In Jesus Name, Amen.

DAY 71
PROVERBS 10:17

17 He [is in] the way of life that keeps instruction: but he that refuses correction errs.

As you grow older you are going to see TV shows and movies of the military doing drills. Maybe one day in the future you may choose to become a part of the military and will take part in drills. Drills in the military prepare you to do two things: to follow orders and prepare you to act instinctually. That means you will act if something happens without even thinking. This drilling saves their lives.

Another way to look at this is the person who takes keyboarding class, something we used to call "Typing." The drills are terribly boring at times. But they teach your fingers where the keys are. They create something called "muscle memory." So, your fingers and brain react know where each letter is and without thinking find the correct key. No hunting for letters, just quickness. Good typists are able to type 60 words a minute. Great typists, type over 100 words a minute.

Now let's look at this as if it is happening to you. Think about learning multiplication tables. You drilled so hard, so that when someone says "3 x 4 ="? You immediately say "12." What would happen if a student told his teacher, "11!" She corrected him telling him it is 12. But he insists he is right and ignores what she tells him. What do you think will happen to him? Will he get 3 x 5 or 3 x 6 correct? Will he learn the rest of his times tables correctly? What about other things in life?

We have to be able to keep what we are taught. We have to respect those who correct us and learn from them. Oh, it is not easy to accept correction sometimes. I guarantee there will be days when someone tells you, you did something wrong and shows you what that is helping you correct it, that you will be totally mad. You won't want to listen. But as Christians we have to be willing to learn. We have to be willing to make ourselves better.

Dear God,

Please mold me into a person who keeps what he learns. Work on my memory, make learning easier for me. Help me to desire to learn even more. I may not love school, but I know You want the best for me and that means I should like learning.

Lord, help me to be kind when I am corrected. Help me to learn from correction that I may become better and be seen as an example of your love to others.

In Jesus Name, Amen.

DAY 72
PROVERBS 10:19

19 In the multitude of words sin is not lacking, But he who restrains his lips [is] wise.

It's amazing how some people can talk and talk while others can be very quiet. It will not be long before you see how those with a lot of words tend to be covering up sin, hiding it. You will also meet people who use words and flowery speech to tempt you to join with them in sin.

In general, the person who has a lot to say is not to be trusted. This does not mean people whose jobs that involve selling or speeches should not be trusted. It means you should watch to see if they should be trusted.

Watch for those who say little also. It takes some wisdom to restrain what you say. This person is the opposite of the fool whose wisdom is soon parted because he does not understand that his words will quickly betray he/she and lack wisdom and understanding.

Think about this. Are there times, you wish you simply kept your mouth shut and did not say something? I know that is true for me. Words once said, that you want to take back, require a lot of work. Sometimes seeking forgiveness is needed. It is so much easier to rest in this: there is wisdom in keeping your mouth shut.

Lord Jesus,

Please help me set a guard about my mouth. Sometimes I so easily say things I should never say. Help me to understand the wisdom of holding my tongue. Help me to keep somethings unsaid that I may be a better example of your love to others.

In Jesus Name, Amen.

DAY 73
PROVERBS 10:20

20 The tongue of the righteous [is] choice silver; The heart of the wicked [is worth] little.

21 The lips of the righteous feed many, But fools die for lack of wisdom.

Believe it or not, there are people who simply get paid for talking. They get hired to talk because their fresh and open honesty is coupled with wisdom. Some of these people get paid only to give speeches. Some of them write also.

On the flip side, the heart of the wicked is usually full of words that include cussing. Sadly, they can't seem to remove the swear words from their vocabulary. They can't seem to keep jobs, because of their wickedness. Some, because of their foolishness risk their own lives daily. Do a search on YouTube of "stupid" and "work" and you will see why.

Lord God,

Help me to seek wisdom, help me Lord, because my own righteousness is not my own, but Yours. It is Your love that saved me. Help me to be an example of what you have done for me. Help me to be a boy who is known for kindness and wisdom. Lord, let my words and deeds stand side by side.

In Jesus Name, Amen.

DAY 74
PROVERBS 10:22

22 The blessing of the LORD, it makes rich, and he add no sorrow with it.

Have you ever heard the saying, "If God gives you lemons, make lemonade". We have a God who understands and knows our needs far beyond our understanding. This God we serve, planned to meet our needs before we had the need. God goes so far as to give us financial blessings. Blessings can make you rich!

You could be blessed with the gift of the ability to talk with anyone. That could be God's way of making you richly blessed with friends. God could gift you with an understanding of math, which could lead to you working for a technology giant. No matter what the blessing, any blessing enriches you! It makes you better.

NO SORROW—no sadness. No wishing you didn't have the blessing that comes from God. Interesting here is that it does not say, you should thank God for your blessings.

Dear Jesus!

Thank you for the many blessings you give me daily. Thank you for the many blessings. Lord, I give you praise for blessings you gave me, and those you will give me in the future.

In Jesus Name Amen.

DAY 75
PROVERBS 10:23

23 [It is] as sport to a fool to do mischief: but a man of understanding hath wisdom.

Mischief or troublemaking is usually done in small groups. I remember getting caught up into the sport aspect of causing and doing trouble. We decided to play a game, no boy should play called, "Ding Dong Ditch." Basically, someone would push a doorbell then disappear before the person opened the door. Oh, we laughed thinking it funny when we irritated someone. We made it competitive and a sport to see who dared to stay the longest before running off, who would ring the bell the most on a house. We didn't think about those who came to the door. We didn't think about how this was bothering them. We only thought of how funny it was then. We didn't think about an older person having to struggle to get up and then come to the door. We didn't care at all for anyone else, only what brought us pleasure.

That is a very selfish way to live. We were encouraging and pushing each other to commit a sin. We never thought of the pain some people experience walking. We didn't think about anything but ourselves and how we could have fun doing this even better, just like playing soccer.

If I had been wise, I may have said no. Mrs. Feen was in her 70s and had difficulty walking. Her sister used a walker. The Feen sisters lived in one of the houses we pranked. There were places where little children were sleeping, and we didn't care that this was one of the only moments that the mother got a well-deserved break. We didn't care that our game caused babies to cry.

Wisdom was leveraged on us when we got caught. A paddling was something we earned.

Wisdom would have kept us from playing the part of the fool. The fool who does not care for others.

Dear Jesus,

Please help me to be a boy who seeks to what is right and not what is foolish. Waken my heart and mind to understand how what I do affects others. Help me to see how important it is too do what is right by you.

In Jesus Name, Amen.

DAY 76
PROVERBS 10:24

24 The fear of the wicked will come upon him, and the desire of the righteous will be granted.

Those who have a heart to do evil have some pretty awful nightmares. They fear the evils they do being done to them. The more evil they are the more paranoid they get. Oh, they hide it well, but it is there. That fear is grounded in reality.

The righteous don't have these fears. Yes, they do have some fears. I am not comfortable in high places. Funny thing considering how high up in trees I used to climb.

But for God---the righteous owe their righteousness to Jesus' sacrifice on the cross for our sins. God is so generous to those who truly seek him. He gives a promise to them—that desires of the righteous will be granted! Imagine prayers being answered easily because you earnestly seek God.

Lord God,

I seek to be Yours. I want You to lead and rule over my life. I want to be counted among the righteous. I want my prayers to be answered as you promise the righteous. Help me to become the bait that others see that they may choose to follow you! Guide my footsteps. Help me to choose what is right.

In Jesus name, Amen.

DAY 77
PROVERBS 10:25

25 As the whirlwind passes, so [is] the wicked no [more]: but the righteous [is] an everlasting foundation.

There is an old saying, "There are no atheists in foxholes." Foxholes are holes that soldiers dig to protect themselves in battle. When the bullets are flying is your faith enough?

During World War II, a man named Deitrich Bonhoeffer was imprisoned in Nazi Germany. Bonhoeffer was a preacher who on the day when Hitler took power was on the radio warning people about the dangers Hitler would bring to the German people.

Bonhoeffer shared Jesus in prison. He shared Jesus both by his example and by his words. What amazed everyone was his calmness. When Germany was being bombed, Bonhoeffer sat calmly praying while others screamed out, fearing death.

His faith in Jesus was a firm foundation. He carried him through the storm of the bombings. Our righteousness is not our own. Our firm foundation is in Jesus.

Lord Jesus,

Help me to be calm in times of trouble. Help me to know you are there and will not me leave me. Build up in me such a faith that others may know You through what they see in me. Let my faith be seen as something that makes many wonder what I have that is so different.

In Jesus Name, Amen.

DAY 78
PROVERBS 10:26

26 As vinegar to the teeth, and as smoke to the eyes, so [is] the sluggard to them that send him.

A sluggard is a person who is lazy. The person who would be sending this person would be a boss, an employer, or a businessman who hired him to do something.

I remembered hearing something about the damage vinegar can do to teeth, so I looked it up. Vinegar can remove the enamel on your teeth. It's possible you may not even know the damage you have done to your teeth until much later. This made me think of how a lazy man can damage a business.

When you need help in a store and a clerk sees you but does not answer your request for help are you willing to shop there again? On the surface, the customer buys something. So, nothing bad is seen. But that customer will not return and will tell others not to go to this business. This could ruin a business!

When smoke gets in your eyes, what do you do? You squint, and you blink. You try to protect your eyes. It irritates your eyes, making what you see difficult and limited.

If you send a lazy man to do something are you trusting him to do something you would do? Do you really have faith in him? The man who sends a lazy man cannot trust him. That businessman cannot plan ahead because he is not sure of what the lazy employee will do. When a business does not plan ahead it plans to fail.

Lord Jesus,

Help me to not be the man people do not trust because of laziness. Help me to not be lazy. Help me to do my chores and homework on time and not need reminders. I want to become a man that is an example of You to others. Work on me and make me into that example!

In Jesus Name, Amen.

DAY 79
PROVERBS 10:27

27 The fear of the LORD prolongs your days: but the years of the wicked shall be shortened.

When God repeats something, it is to communicate something important. In Proverbs, we find that He repeats several things saying them in different ways. As a young student you might think about how your teacher says somethings over and over again before you get it.

God is a patient teacher. He lets us make mistakes. He watches us stumble and is there to help us when we are ready to stand back up.

This proverb is simple. If we love God and honor Him with our words and deeds He will prolong our days. This could mean He sends angels to help guard you from harm. He watches over us in so many ways. Keeping harm from us seems so small a task for Him.

It can also mean our days are prolonged because we are saved by Jesus and we will be with Him in Heaven one day. We will live with Him in the place he prepared for us.

The "years of the wicked being shortened" reminds me of how many sins come with physical ailments. Things that good men and women of God who follow His wisdom never get. Wickedness is its own reward. It is short sighted. It does not see the prize at following Jesus. It only sees the immediate future.

Dear God,

Help me to seek after you. Help me to be a young man who follows after you with my heart, my words, and my actions. I want to be the one who draws others to you by being an example. Please work on me and make a better example of you.

Lord, please help me to draw those who do not know You from their wickedness to a desire to serve You.

In Jesus Name, Amen.

DAY 80
PROVERBS 10:28

28 The hope of the righteous [shall be] gladness: but the expectation of the wicked shall perish.

One of the most important questions today that needs to be asked of everyone is, "Where is your hope?"

The Atheists place their hope in a better future on this earth for them alone. Some place their hope in working their way to heaven. They will say their hope is in being good enough to get into heaven. Their hope is short-sighted. It is in what they can do for themselves.

The hope of the believer is in Christ Jesus, who gave His life for us that we may have eternal life. He paid the price for our sin.

Our hope is in the living God! We hope in His promises!

Dear Jesus!

Thank you for being my hope! Thank you for all you have done for me and you will do for me. I rest in your strong fortress of hope for what lies beyond this world.

Help me to draw others to you Lord Jesus, so that they too may share in the joy and hope of knowing You!

In Jesus Name, Amen.

DAY 81
PROVERBS 10:29

29 The way of the LORD [is] strength to the upright: but destruction [shall be] to the workers of sin.

This is something I was just talking about last night. God wants us to do what is right. The cool thing is the promises for you if you do what is right and place God first in your life. Then following and doing what he says, can become easier. How is this possible? When you start to learn something, you make mistakes. But eventually you catch on. You create a pattern of behavior called a habit. Doing what is right so much that it becomes part of who you are can become strength and encouragement to continue in doing what is right. Why is it strength? It becomes second nature. You don't have to think about should I do this which is sinful or do what God wants me to do. You naturally choose God.

Sadly, the person who chooses to become a "worker of sin" usually chooses to do something illegal and works at doing the

120

illegal activity. They become "better sinners." They work on the sin they want to commit over and over. Most sins have a penalty attached. Not just the time or fine you get for breaking the law. Many sins have sickness and disease attached to them. Some of these illnesses lead to death. Alcoholics destroy their liver. Smokers destroy their lungs. Drug addiction destroys parts of their brain and their heart.

Lord Jesus,

Thank you for your many promises for doing what is right. You are my strong tower, my refuge in my time of need. You make my life easier by strengthening me in what I do that is Your will.

Lord, please keep me from sinful ways. Lead me away from the temptations that would lead me to destruction. Help me to make You and my parents proud.

In Jesus Name, Amen.

DAY 82
PROVERBS 10:30

30 The righteous will never be removed, But the wicked will not inhabit the earth.

Promises by God are always kept. No matter how hard it may seem, our God does impossible things.

This promise tells us no matter how bad things get, no matter how awful life gets, God is still in control! He will not leave us alone!

The wicked—those seeking evil shall not be allowed to possess the land. They are but a passing short-lived problem for us. Their wickedness can impact us severely, but the promise of God is that their time is short compared to that of the righteous.

This Proverb tells us how to pray when there is someone wicked ruling, whether they serve in an office of power or as employer. We are to pray about God's promise of their time being brief—short. When we pray this, we are to pray the righteous become the replacement of the wicked. When France had its revolution, they went from one wicked ruler to another who was more wicked. We need to be the long-sighted and pray for righteous leaders to rule over us. The Bible tells us to pray for those who rule over us. So, this should be part of your daily prayers. Pray for those in office like the President, the Governor, and the Mayor. If they are what you believe is wicked, pray they find Jesus or that God quickly removes them since he promised that the wicked shall not inhabit the earth.

Dear Jesus,

I thank You for Your many promises to me. Your promise here tells me You will never leave me alone. You are always here watching over me. You are my strong tower. My refuge in time of need. You open your arms and wait for me to run to you to melt into them as your child.

Lord, Your love for me emboldens me. It makes me excited knowing You will stand with us. Since everything in this world passes, if something will never be removed it is because You protect it! God use me. Use me as an example to draw many to You.

In Jesus Name, Amen.

DAY 83
PROVERBS 10:31-32

31 From the mouth of the righteous comes the fruit of wisdom, but a perverse tongue will be silenced.

32 The lips of the righteous know what finds favor, but the mouth of the wicked only what is perverse.

Maybe it is because I teach in the city, maybe not, but—I am constantly having to deal with students who have foul mouths. I am not very patient listening to someone cuss. It makes me angry to hear someone cuss when talking to me, whether they are cussing at me or simply swearing. It's a sign of disrespect! Worse, it is a sign of a lack of creativity.

Those who cuss regularly seem to find those same wards all the time. You know what I am saying is true! They almost never stretch to find something better to describe what they mean. They never attempt to paint what they are saying with more descriptive words. The cut straight to cussing.

In a classroom you can see how quickly the person who cusses is silenced. They either stop or they end up in the principal's office! Worse, they can end up going home!

But what about the person with kind words? What about the boy who thinks before he speaks? What about the person who listens, and when he talks you wait to hear his/her thoughts? They found favor in your heart, right?

Now, if the person who cusses regularly finds favor in your heart, unless they are your mom or other family member, maybe your heart should not be following them. You want to be the one who sets the example to draw others unto Jesus right? If you want this, you need to be the one who controls his tongue. You want to be the one others want to hear because they know your words are kind and true. If you are hanging out with people like this, your brain will eventually pick up cussing and repeat it. The truth is that being Christian means being different in how we appear to others. We can't use cussing because we are pretty sure, Jesus, never would cuss! Some people think Jesus never got angry so how could he understand what it means to be angry. Yet when Jesus saw men cheating each other in the Temple, it angered Him so much he grabbed a whip and chased them out of there! He used words that corrected and rebuked. Not one of them cussed!

Be different! Stand out! Choose to be the one whose words convey wisdom, not cusses!

Lord Jesus,

Please set a guard over my mouth. I know myself, I think about saying things I should never let pass through my lips if I want to be an example of You! Lord work on me, make others see my choice to follow you, by the words I choose to express myself.

Lord Jesus, please help me to choose my words wisely when I am angry. Help me to think about how others see me when I am angry. I should never embarrass my parents or You in the words that pass through my lips. Thank You Lord, for helping me with this.

In Jesus name, Amen.

DAY 84
PROVERBS 11:1

11 Dishonest scales are an abomination to the Lord, but a just weight is His delight.

In Bible times and even today, a lot of things are sold by their weight. Things like seed or grain are sold by weight. That's how gold is sold, too. The food we buy has the weight of it on the can, jar or bottle. Today weighting is done with digital scales. During Bible times, merchants had their own scales. Some were right and honest. While others cheated those who were buying. Those kinds of scales, the Lord hated. Yet He loved those who never cheated their customers. If you were going into business, you should do what is right by your customers. The Lord likes that, and those customers will tell others of your honesty.

Father,

If I ever try to sell something, let me do it the right way and at the right value, because I know that this pleases You.

I pray and thank You in Jesus name. Amen.

DAY 85
PROVERBS 11:2

2 When pride comes, then comes shame; But with the humble is wisdom.

Pride is known as one of the 7 deadly sins! It is very dangerous! It also must be avoided. Why? Because you can be hurt by it. Maybe not physically hurt, yet in other ways. You may speak out of turn and you are scolded for it. You might do something you were repeatedly told not to do. You can get punished for being prideful, because you didn't listen the first or second time. Both of these examples are embarrassing. That's where the shame comes in. The humble hardly sees this. Because they have and use wisdom. This causes them to avoid much trouble. Will you use the wisdom you have?

Father,

I thank You for Your Word that helps me to do what is right. Please add to the wisdom You have given me. Please help me to use the wisdom I already have. To keep myself and others from trouble or even danger.

I pray and thank You in Jesus name. Amen.

DAY 86
PROVERS 11:3

3 The integrity of the upright will guide them, but the perversity of the unfaithful will destroy them.

The honesty of those trying to live right will direct them. It will show them how to keep doing the right they're doing. It will also show them what to stay away from.

The foolishness of those who can't stay right will tear them down. This is not good.

God doesn't want to see us go that way. He wants us to do what is good and right, so we can enjoy life more. Sounds like a plan?

Father,

Please help me to be faithful to You. Help me to live by what You say. Help me not to change my mind from You. Help me not to do things that will tear me down.

I pray and thank You in Jesus name. Amen.

DAY 87
PROVERBS 11:4

Riches do not profit in the day of wrath, but righteousness delivers from death.

When serious trouble comes your way, no amount of money can save you. This reminds me of a scene from a movie. A desperate businessman gave a bus driver two $100 bills! Traffic was jammed. Everyone was trying to leave at the same time. Why? Because a massive flood of water was coming their way! Right then that $200 was meaningless! Because they both died where they were! On the other hand, being right with God can deliver us from trouble. Being right with God can save us from death if we keep following Him.

Father,

Please help me not to set my heart on money. Only let my heart be on You where it belongs, for money doesn't help every situation. Yet, You can and You will help me to know this more. Please help me to trust You more.

I pray and thank You in Jesus name. Amen.

DAY 88
PROVERBS 11:5

5 The righteousness of the blameless will direct his way aright, but the wicked will fall by his own wickedness.

Again, the honesty of those who continue to do right will guide them. What you find right to do, you will hopefully want to keep doing; Like the simple pleasure of pleasing God and making your parents happy. Yet, those who choose to keep doing wrong will pay for it - often a heavy price at that. They can be hurt, or worse. God does not want that for you. He wants you to choose the right way, and to stay on it! Can you do that? Will you do that for Him and for yourself?

Father,

Please help me to live the way You want me to. Help me to always choose what is good and right. Help me to please You with what I do and say.

I pray and thank You in Jesus name. Amen.

DAY 89
PROVERBS 11:6

6 The righteousness of the upright will deliver them,
But the unfaithful will be caught by their lust.

As long as we try to do the right thing, that can keep us safe. Life can be full of trouble. The Bible says so. We don't need to add any more of that to it. This is not so for the unfaithful - those who don't fully trust and believe the Lord. Those who want their own way all the time without listening to wisdom or good advice. These people are always in trouble. They also have a hard time getting out of it. Only God can help them at this point. They must first choose to do right. And follow His way out through His Word.

———————⋯———————

Father,

Please help me to do what is right. And not to add any more trouble to my life. By doing any wrong. Help me to listen when I am told what is right, by You and by my parents, and others who care about me. Help me to do the right thing to keep myself and others safe.

I pray and thank You in Jesus name. Amen.

DAY 90
PROVERBS 11:8

8 The righteous is delivered from trouble,
And it comes to the wicked instead.

———————⋯———————

An example of this happened to me just the other day. I was driving home from the mountains. Two pick-up trucks decided to drive very close to me almost on my bumper. I was getting upset. People know they cause trouble when they do this to other drivers. Suddenly they decided to go around me. At the same time, a deer started to run across the highway. Quickly the truck drivers put on their brakes! I smiled. Knowing that the deer was no accident. Because it was at the right place and at the right time to show those truck drivers how foolish they were! Thanks God!

———————⋯———————

Father God,
Thank You for protecting me. Thank You for always being there when I need you. You are so faithful. Please help me to believe Your promises to me even more.

I pray and thank You in Jesus name. Amen.

DAY 92
PROVERBS 11:9

The hypocrite with his mouth destroys his neighbor,
But through knowledge the righteous will be delivered.

    Words are very powerful. Using the wrong yet strong ones can always hurt someone. Once they are out there, you can't take them back. One who is a hypocrite can never be trusted because he or she cannot hold onto what they believe. They believe their own lies, and expect others to believe them, too. Stay away from people like this. Yet the righteous can be spared or delivered. Why? Because they know and believe the truth. Knowing the truth, they can easily spot a lie coming at them. May we seek to be this wise.

Father God,
Please help me to stay away from hypocrites - those who don't believe as I do, and are always speaking lies. Help me to know the difference between Your truth and a lie. Help me to live in Your truth alone.

I pray and thank You in Jesus name. Amen.

DAY 93
PROVERBS 11:10

When it goes well with the righteous, the city rejoices;

And when the wicked perish, there is jubilation.

There is great joy when good people win. When people believe God and do what He says, and they see the result of listening and obeying Him. He blesses their obedience. This makes everyone who knows Him very glad, like when Jesus would go to a town and heal people. The town would be excited because they saw their prayers being answered by Him. This is enough to make any city happy! There is also another kind of joy. When someone who is bad dies. Those who are still alive and remain can now enjoy peace, once this evil person is out of the way. Life can always be better when bad people are gone. Would you agree?

Father God,
Please help me to be and stay right with You, in all I do and say. Help me to be glad, with the city, when good people win. Guide me to be one of those good people. Teach me to trust in You and do what You tell me.

I pray and thank You in Jesus name. Amen.

DAY 94
PROVERBS 11:11

By the blessing of the upright the city is exalted,
But it is overthrown by the mouth of the wicked.

When God's people do well, the city is held in high honor. It is respected more because of those who do what is right. On the other hand, when people talk bad about a city, it suffers. A friend of mine always gave a bad name to our city, as did others. When angry with it, I called it the same thing I must confess.

"Rottenchester" was the word used to describe what was wrong with this city. When enough people hear you talk bad about your own city, why would they come, or even want to? That's how a city can be overthrown - by the bad things said about it. Let's not be that way. Instead of being part of the problem, we should be part of the solution. How? By praying to God to fix what's wrong. And to help us to do what we can to make it better!

Father God,
I pray for my city. That You would help fix what is wrong, so there is less fighting and less accidents. I pray for people to care more for one another, and for more people to help make it better.

I pray and thank You in Jesus name. Amen.

DAY 95
PROVERBS 11:12

He who is devoid of wisdom despises his neighbor,
But a man of understanding holds his peace.

"Devoid" means completely empty, which means someone who hates his neighbor doesn't have much sense. My neighbor used to play his music loud in his apartment under me. That made it hard for me to sleep after work. I must confess I started to dislike him a lot because of this. That all changed when I got my car stuck in the snow! I was back home from work. I tried to pull into the driveway. The snow was too deep. I got stuck in it! My neighbor without thinking began pushing on my car to help me get out. I was amazed and glad. I thanked him when it was over, and my attitude changed about him. A man of understanding or wisdom holds his peace when he knows that blowing his top can make the situation worse. Have you held your peace when you had to? Have you said nothing even though you felt like it?

———————◦———————

Father God,
Thank You for Your wise words to help me live right and to live good. Help me not to dislike anyone, because I never know when I may need that same person. Please help me to forgive quickly when someone hurts me. Help me to keep quiet when I should not say nothing.

I pray and thank You in Jesus name. Amen.

DAY 96
PROVERBS 11:13

A talebearer reveals secrets,
But he who is of a faithful spirit conceals a matter.

———————◦———————

Ever see anyone gossip? This is someone telling another person about someone else's business. This is not cool. It also can be very embarrassing depending on what it is. I hope you are never this type of person. This can turn family and friends against each other. That is never a good thing. Yet if you are wise and faithful, you can keep things to yourself as long as it is not harmful to anyone. As the saying goes, "some things are better left unsaid". This is very true. Especially when there's a chance of someone being hurt. Don't be a talebearer or a tattletale. Try being a good listener and a true friend. Sound like a plan?

———————◦———————

Father God,
Please help me to keep things to myself when I need to. Don't let me share anyone's secrets and embarrass them. Please help me

to be a good listener and a true friend. And even pray with
them.

I pray and thank You in Jesus name. Amen.

DAY 97
PROVERBS 11:14

Where there is no counsel, the people fall;
But in the multitude of counselors there is safety.

―――――――――――――――

Like sheep, people need guidance. We have to be shown where to go and how to get there safely. God understood this. This is why He gave us His Word. It is also why He gave us Jesus. He wanted to show us the way. Because He is The Truth, The Way and The Life. Always remember this because He was and still is our best example in dealing with problems, people and life in general! Without Him, we fall. Without using His wisdom from the Word, we fail. Yet when we listen to Him, to our parents, and our teachers, we can win. We can also be and stay safe. Amen!

―――――――――――――――

Father,
Please help me to listen for Your counsel. Through Your Word, from Your Holy Spirit, my parents, pastors and teachers. Help me to use it and use it well. Because I know it can and will help me to win!

In Jesus name I pray and thank You. Amen.

DAY 98
PROVERBS 11:15

15 He who is surety for a stranger will suffer,

But one who hates being surety is secure.

This is a definite word of wisdom. Surety means taking responsibility for someone else. This takes a lot of thought. Most people have a problem doing this for friends. Even for some family members. Yet to take responsibility for a stranger is next to impossible. If you are wise, you will allow them to find someone else. There is peace in that. Not taking on someone else's problems. They can be here today and gone tomorrow, with you holding the bag as they say! 2000 years ago, Jesus was surety for you and me. We were headed for a great and horrible punishment for our sins. Jesus stepped in and became surety for us. Taking responsibility for every bad and wrong thing we have done on Himself. Why did He do it? Because of His great love for us. As it is written in Romans 5:8, "while we were still sinners, Christ died for us." So, we should always be thankful for that - grateful He took our place when we deserved to be punished.

Dear Lord Jesus,

Thank You for becoming surety for me - taking my place from being punished by God. Thank You for shedding Your blood for me, and making me right with the Father. Help me to prove how grateful I am, by living right and living for You.

In Your name I pray and thank You. Amen.

Made in United States
North Haven, CT
26 April 2024

51772910R00082